Lost For Words
Language and Educational Failure

J. W. Patrick Creber

Lost For Words
Language and Educational Failure

J. W. Patrick Creber

Penguin Books
in association with the National Association
for the Teaching of English

Penguin Books Ltd, Harmondsworth,
Middlesex, England
Penguin Books Inc, 7110 Ambassador Road,
Baltimore, Md 21207, USA
Penguin Books Australia Ltd,
Ringwood, Victoria, Australia

First published 1972
Reprinted 1973
Copyright © J. W. Patrick Creber and the National
Association for the Teaching of English, 1972

Made and printed in Great Britain by
C. Nicholls & Company Ltd
Set in Linotype Granjon

Contents

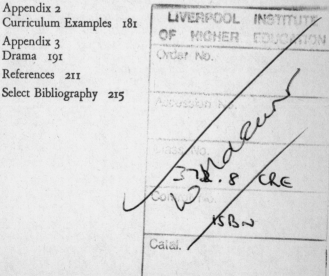

Acknowledgements

In the writing of this book I have been supported and encouraged by the perceptive advice and criticism of many friends. My particular thanks are due to Leslie Stratta, and also to Tony Edwards, Geoffrey Fox, Harold and Connie Rosen, Andrew Wilkinson, Bob Turner, Martin Lightfoot and to Gill, my wife.

Preface

This book has its origin in the Anglo-American Seminar held
in July 1968, under the auspices of the National Association
for the Teaching of English and supported by a grant from
the Gulbenkian Foundation, at the West Midlands College of
Education, Walsall. At this – the 'Walsall Seminar' to which
I shall frequently refer – over forty teachers from all kinds of
schools and colleges in Britain and America, as well as
administrators and inspectors, spent twelve days discussing the
linguistic problems of those young people who in the eyes of
school or society are failures.

While the general problems of these 'dropouts' had received
considerable publicity in recent years, participants at the seminar
felt the need to draw attention more specifically to the place of
language in learning and hence to the effects of linguistic
impoverishment, however caused, upon school performance.
Had the Seminar concerned itself only with the plight of a
minority suffering exceptional handicaps, the need for publicity
might have seemed less pressing, but though discussion at
first centred on the problems in their more obvious and extreme
forms, it rapidly broadened to embrace aspects of the curriculum
affecting far more pupils than those relatively small groups that
could be labelled subnormal, backward or in need of remedial
teaching. It is the breadth of the implications for the curriculum
of *many* pupils that is the justification of this book.

The Schools Council Working Paper no. 27, *Cross'd with
Adversity* (1970), illustrates by eloquent case histories
something of the range of problems of deprivation, but admits
also that 'there are grounds for believing that many, perhaps
most, children need some form of compensation' (p. 8).
Later on, it speaks of 'a hidden drag on many a seemingly
average child's school career' (p. 45). I shall want not merely

to support this idea but to relate it quite specifically to linguistic deprivation, which is to be seen as a continuum rather than as the peculiar affliction of a small minority. To interpret the 'hidden drag' in this way will involve consideration of more than language alone, however. By looking at those contexts at home and school where the child acquires, more or less successfully, the linguistic tools that he needs, I shall hope to shed some light on the complex interplay of social, psychological and linguistic factors within the learning process.

The need for such an approach is outlined in chapter one. Chapter two looks at some of the evidence on language development that may help us to assess current and projected educational practice. This evaluation is attempted in the subsequent chapters, three being concerned with relatively traditional teaching situations and four with more recent trends and developments. The final chapter examines the implications of the survey for the future, particularly as these affect teacher training.

I *Cause for Concern*

The organizer pointed to the group I was in. 'Group B will be in room 22'.

A few moments later we were there, seated, expectant, notebooks ready. A small brisk man entered. He looked at us briefly, smiled and began to speak. In Urdu.

It was 9.30 a.m. and coffee was not until 11. The door was shut. I suddenly realized that he was repeating something and pointing at me. Having no idea what he was saying, and fearing that he might by some oriental magic have divined my thoughts, I did the only thing possible – tried to repeat what he had said. He smiled and nodded; I felt relieved and absurdly grateful.

Patiently employing every device of repetition and gesture to amplify his meaning, he went on until everyone had made some stumbling attempt. And then another round of questions while our confidence began to grow. After an hour and a half we felt wrung out.

These shock tactics, described by a member of a group of teachers of English as a foreign language on a training weekend, may have led to the learning of a few useful phrases but its main object – that the teacher should share something of the predicament of the immigrant child – was certainly achieved. The teacher's knowledge of the child's country, culture, family life and language, is likely to remain largely sterile unless informed by feeling and imagination.

We have too long assumed that we could affect language use by intellectual instruction alone, we have isolated it from other aspects of personal and social behaviour and development. To meditate upon the teacher's account above is to see something of the complexity of such behaviour – it is perhaps surprising to some that a 'grown man' should feel *grateful* (he was himself surprised by it), but others who have felt the social exposure that accompanies language ignorance will not be surprised.

If an adult may be expected to feel exposed when placed in

an alien (not necessarily a foreign) language environment, we need to ponder the thoughts and feelings, in a similarly exposed position, of a child who by comparison with the majority of his peers has suffered emotional, material or cultural deprivation. How does such a 'disadvantaged' child feel when confronted, not merely with the language of his more fortunate contemporaries but with the conventional utterances of teachers, with those styles of language in which school education is normally conducted? We shall see, when we come to consider the classroom situation, just some of the problems which the child must face.

The teacher on that training course was interested in the problems of immigrant, mostly black, children; my concern is with indigenous, mostly grey, children, and it will be part of my argument that myopic teachers and administrators don't notice grey kids as easily as black ones, or, if they notice them, they may assume that they speak the same language as these children – a serious delusion, as I shall hope to show. At the Walsall Seminar on the 'Language of Failure' the plight of our grey children became more real to us as we listened to teachers who had worked in areas of extreme deprivation. Thus Paul Widlake, then Adviser on Remedial Education in Wolverhampton:

The children are sometimes unkempt and often (but by no means always) emotionally deprived. The discipline in the home is likely to be unstable, veering from excessive punishment to easy-going indifference. The children show an imbalance in intelligence test scores, frequently showing better results on non-verbal than on verbal scales. Their attention span may be very brief and, in early learning situations, they may reveal a lack of auditory discrimination because of the lack of opportunity for quiet listening in the home. They may value physical prowess more than intellectual; but more likely they will show a marked lack of curiosity, an unwillingness to explore new situations. Cognitively they reflect their run-down physical condition. I worked for eighteen months in the poorest of such schools in a Midland borough. In one group there was a little boy who always appeared in such a condition that my first action was to hand him a paper tissue. I became completely ruthless abut it; that nose had to be cleaned. One day he was wriggling more than usual and on inspection, proved to be one mass of flea bites; one of the visitors transferred itself to me, the rest I sent home for remediation. In another group there was a child who had been badly burned through parental neglect. Many of the children were unsure of their identity and had had experience of a number of men occupying the position of father-figure. Among the older children, both boys and girls, incestuous assaults by either parent are horrifyingly common.

Another participant at the seminar, Kathleen Browning, who teaches in Charlestown, West Virginia, painted a picture that was broadly similar:

The discerning teacher who is able to identify with the child or understand his problems will be able to look at the mud on his shoes and realize there is probably no sidewalk where he lives; there is no family car which delivers him to school in the morning and picks him up after school. Further visualization by the teacher can picture a cold house where the student lives; bare or linoleum-covered floors; twenty-five watt, dangling light bulbs; dirty and torn wallpaper; soiled, dilapidated furniture; not enough hot water for baths or washing dishes; no privacy; one towel used by the whole family; one drinking cup or glass for the whole family; no reading material; few clean clothes; and perhaps alcoholic parents who are constantly quarrelling over food, money – just anything! There is usually a television set which is on, but that is probably better than dead silence or angry words. The child may not get his share of the family food unless he is there when the food is ready, and at the table he is told to 'shut up and eat', for mealtime is not the family affair it is in middle-class homes. Swearing may be practically the only communication among family members, and 'damn' may be inseparable from the preface 'god' in their minds. 'Go to hell' is interiorized in many families in the United States as 'bloody' and 'bleeding' seem to be for some of the British. Slapping and whipping is the common form of discipline used daily and indiscriminately for minor infractions or serious misdeeds, based on the 'spare the rod and spoil the child' philosophy. Some students never have a chance to talk much or to have anyone listen or try to understand them. . . .
The story is told that in one of our Head Start programs for preschool children in West Virginia, a teacher mentioned to a mother that her child needed a bath, and the mother replied, 'You're supposed to larn 'em, not smell 'em.'

It is true that the general features of grey culture have recently been attracting a deeper and more sympathetic analysis than ever before, but often the root problems seem so deep-seated and insoluble as to invite despair, since to remedy them would convulse society. As Sir Alec Clegg asks, how long will it be before children can divorce their parents?

This growing awareness of the deprivation of sections of our community is reflected in the rapid extension of a vocabulary of deprivation* – it is as if by generating labels to describe deprivation phenomena we sought to convince ourselves that we were doing something about it; that we were not inactive, not unconcerned. Undoubtedly some action is being taken, though the problems are daunting, including action within our schools. Even here, however, it is a testimony to some of our basic uncertainties that we feel the need to describe our activities with a specious positiveness – not as remedial teaching (old hat) but as 'Compensatory Education'.

Often such activity seems too pragmatic, however; we are like misguided general practitioners obsessed with removing the symptoms of unknown diseases. I believe Professor Bernstein is right to have misgivings about Compensatory Education, not because of its content – though we might well be wary of the dignified label, might suspect it as a cloak mantling the inanities of a series of expedients – but because it may be distracting us from our responsibility to review the whole field of language work in school, and to provide an adequate *initial* educational environment. Citing the statistics of the Newsom Report, which showed 79 per cent of the secondary modern schools in slum and problem areas as grossly inadequately staffed and equipped, Bernstein says

I do not understand how we can talk about offering compensatory education to children who in the first place have not, as yet, been offered an adequate educational environment (Bernstein, 1970, p. 111).

In the provision of such an environment, my concern is with one aspect of deprivation, where action is possible, namely lan-

*A point made splendidly by the captions to a Feiffer cartoon: 'I used to think I was poor. Then they told me I wasn't poor, I was *needy*. Then they told me it was self-defeating to think of myself as *needy*, I was deprived. Then they told me *deprived* was a bad image, I was *underprivileged*. Then they told me under-privileged was over-used, I was *disadvantaged*. I still don't have a dime. But I have a great vocabulary.'

gauge. The relationship between general and linguistic impoverishment, and the base on which the school has to build, are suggested by one head teacher:

We have children starting school for whom the words one, two, three, four, five, represent a new language, children who are so unawakened to the world around them that the meaning of the colour words, red, blue, etc., is not known. Of the nineteen children admitted in September this year there are eight who could not fit red to a red jersey or blue to a blue bead. Looking at a book, having someone read a story from it, or talk to them about it, is a new experience, as is the handling of a pencil or crayon (Clegg and Megson, 1968, p. 47).

This is hard to conceive, but the situation may be little better on entry to the secondary school where one can find children – not even 'educationally subnormal' – unable to fill in the simplest form with details of name, school, home address and sex.

For some people's money this is proof positive of what they've always said – that kids just fool around in school nowadays. Facts are still felt to be what education is about; the mind is a cupboard that should not be bare. If some advertisers woo us with the opportunity to increase our word-power, the implication of improved social and professional proficiency is not misleading, though the pre-packaged method may be. Our secondary-modern child is not just short on fact, nor on words; he lacks a social and verbal environment in which words are used to make sense of experience: to share it; to celebrate it; to play with it; to mull it over; to accompany action; to think with.

If it is hard to imagine what school must feel like to an immigrant child, it is not much easier to put oneself in the place of our own, grey, children. I can still recall vividly the impression made on me, as a student-teacher, by B. M. Spinley's book, *The Deprived and the Privileged* (1953). This is an early study of what sociologists call subcultures, one deprived, set in a slum area of East London, the other privileged, associated with a particular public school. It was not the comparison that caught my interest, however, but the account of the deprived area in which the author had lived for several months to carry out her observations. In this section she lists the features of the environment, the home, the parent–child relationships, the prevailing attitudes (e.g. to children, to school, to work, to love, to sex). The picture thus painstakingly built up is strikingly compelling, so that the emergence from such a background of any remotely 'normal' being seems something to marvel at. Even now, after years of teaching in urban industrial areas, I cannot easily imagine what home life is really like in a poor part of Wolverhampton, let alone the Appalachians. Something of the way in which this life is *radically* different is suggested in an article by Peter Lesser (1969), one of whose pupils wrote – 'I used to live with my Mum and her husband and now I live with my Dad and his wife.' Though such a home life may be hard to imagine, it is true that we are now much more aware of problems of social background. I doubt, however, whether this growing awareness extends to the elementary linguistic difficulties that children – often from much less obviously deprived backgrounds – have to face in school.

David, aged eight and a half, and recently passed back from remedial class as being able to read, worked hard at his reading book. One story was about a kindly woodcutter who came across an injured bear and took pity on it. As a result of his ministrations it was healed, only to change into a princess whom the woodcutter, being an adaptable man, fell in love with and married. A simple moral tale, one might think, but not for David. When he was asked to retell it later he introduced the idea that the bear had been chopped into little pieces by the woodcutter. This meant that the happy ending, which he retained in his version, was manifestly nonsensical – a dilemma he was aware of but unable to resolve.

In the present instance not only could the teacher easily have written David off, but like innumerable colleagues in similar situations she could have justified so doing on the grounds that forty other children were demanding attention and that if one attended to every inexplicable kind of individual behaviour one would never teach anyone anything. David's teacher found time, however, to investigate and compare his version of the story with the original. On looking with him at the point where the two accounts diverged she came upon the words – 'the wood-cutter saw the brown bear'.

All was now clear. 'Saw' as the past tense of the verb *to see* had, she realized, no place in David's dialect: if he saw something yesterday he would report 'I *seen* it'. In his dialect 'saw' would only denote an activity associated with precisely such people as woodcutters.

Along with difficulties arising from differing dialects, reading problems may be aggravated by a poverty of conceptual experience so that words are readable but the ideas behind them inconceivable. It comes as a shock to discover a Birmingham nine year old who has never seen a railway station, let alone a farm. The middle-class life-mode and the range of experience with which many 'readers' deal ensure that the impoverished child has to struggle with unpictureable things as well as hard-to-read words. This is hardly surprising since until recently the writing of school readers has been a middle-class employment, so that they have reflected not merely the language but also the attitudes and assumptions of one section of society. This was borne in on me as I visited primary schools in depressed urban areas. The eagerness was remarkable, even pathetic; given the least encouragement, they queued up for me to hear them read. Strident and unkempt, these children haltingly retailed stories that were nearly as incomprehensible as they were dull – haltingly, but with enormous willingness. A few, mostly Pakistani girls, read with enormous fluency and almost total incomprehension. For the middle-class child, who talks naturally of 'Mummy' and 'Daddy' with whom he goes shopping, *en famille,* or on excursions armed with picnic baskets, pets and all the ancillary paraphernalia, the reader may deal with a world which is recognizable. But for children like David, the reader deals in strange words with a strange world, and with parents who behave in ways quite unlike those of the parents he knows – scarcely less strange to him, in fact, than they are to his friend from Pakistan.

If this problem of 'suitable reading material' is serious at primary level, it may be immeasurably more so in the secondary school where one knows of cases where remedial reading practice is given to adolescents; here they may find themselves forced to read in alien, infantile language about the life of *very young middle-class* children. At both levels, however, the nature of the problem is becoming recognized and a small supply of more suitable reading matter becoming available; the smallness of the supply reflects no lack of concern but rather the difficulty of writing for disadvantaged kids in a way that seems real to them and is free from the middle-class condescension of playing at understanding ragamuffins. There is hope, too, in the widespread and justified demand that teachers be better prepared for the teaching of reading, at all levels.

It is no part of my argument to suggest that there are easy answers to such problems. There is room, however, for some decisive ground-clearing operations and there are sources of error and confusion which are removable. For instance, the term 'playground English', sometimes used to denote a kind of language of which teachers disapprove, is now no longer useful for purposes of objective description and can only testify to a misunderstanding of the real problem. The language of the playground is not a speech mode which results from freedom, lack of breeding, of discipline or of self-control; rather is it the language the children encounter in their home or street. Thus the child who defends himself – 'I never bloody swore, sir!' – is expressing, a shade truculently perhaps, what is a truth for him. If the teacher shows himself incapable of understanding this, he is 'a silly fucker', which is not just a swear-word but a word carrying an emotional tone which the child needs to defend himself against a disapproval which may be as violent as it is, to him, incomprehensible. I remember my wife being rebuked for a very mild expression of disapproval of his language by a tough and highly unacademic adolescent: 'Christ, Miss, you'd be dead in a week in the navy!'

To argue that schools should be broader-minded about language, not have their policies dominated by obsessive concerns with respectability or – in a very superficial sense – with morality, is not to deny that they retain a protective function, nor is it to suggest that all standards are meaningless. We do need, however, to revise our priorities: for example to discriminate between morality and what have been called linguistic table-manners. This will involve a rethinking of the relationship between the school and the surrounding community and in this connection the description of parent–school cooperation in Michael Young and Patrick McGeeney's *Learning Begins at Home* (1968) offers some hopeful pointers. A wise ecclesiastic once said that being shocked was a sign of spiritual pride, not of tender virtue. It seems as if schools have sometimes fallen into this trap in their attitude to the surrounding community, its speech and its values. Certainly there has been too often an effort to keep the school somehow inviolate — uncontaminated by the smut all around. And because it is based upon inadequate sympathy and understanding, this effort is likely to be sterile. It is hard to protect any child if you disapprove of him. When he says: 'Well, Miss, 'e pissed off round the corner an' went ass-avatip in t' sandpit!' — what reaction might one expect from a teacher to this vivid communication? A glint of appreciative humour? Such a reaction is rare in schools where teachers attend, not to the message the child is seeking to convey, but to the formal or surface characteristics of the language he uses to convey it.

I hope enough has been said to suggest what the child from a 'poor background' has to face in his early schooling. For David, as for an immigrant, the first days at school will bring an encounter with a culture that is as alien as it is embattled. There have been several moving accounts of this clash written in the past few years. Herbert Kohl (1968) in a slum school in Harlem discovered that there was experience and vitality awaiting release in some of the most apathetic children he taught. He learnt also that to explore such avenues was not the way to endear himself to the establishment.* The opposition is epitomized by the two poems that follow: the first was from an anthology which these slow-learning, 'apathetic' twelve year olds put together with care and pride when they realized that he took their experience seriously —

The Junkies
When they are
in the street
they pass it
along to each
other but when
they see the
police they would

___

* Mr Christopher Searle (1971) made the same discovery in this country. His dismissal is reported in the *Guardian*, 28 May 1971.

run some would
just stand still
and be beat
and so pity ful
that they want
to cry.
(*Marie*)

The second poem was adduced by the school principal and Mrs Bonnett – a tough Negro teacher who acted as his mouthpiece – as part of their campaign to show the apparently obtuse Mr Kohl, and his class, the error of their ways. The poem was amongst work by another (more successful and more socially advantaged) class. Mrs Bonnett smiled kindly as she administered the necessary rebuke: newspapers and magazines weren't for 'that type of nonsense' (junkies, fighting, etc.). But there was no reason Mr Kohl's class couldn't produce something like the flawlessly typed (and teacher-edited) sheet she held up. They were to listen to it, so that they would 'know how to do better'.

Shop with Mom
I love to shop with Mom
And talk to the friendly grocer,
And help her make the list,
Seems to make us closer.
(*Pamela*)
(Kohl, 1968, p. 160)

I do not want to imply that in their reactions to the children's own world, whether it be expressed in the form of a poem about something distasteful or in playground English raising its disreputable head in the classroom, teachers in Britain or America are merely bowing to external pressures. Certainly the fear of social disapproval may modify or even inhibit the teacher's natural response to the child, but this is not the whole story. If a teacher rejects something like the Junkies poem he rejects it because his own social and literary formation – his own conditioning if you like – leads him to do so. Self-reappraisal, of the kind modern techniques make necessary, is a painful, even an agonizing business.

Most of us like to feel secure and this is rarely easy for teachers in poor or in problem areas. The child's language may be seen as carrying with it a threat to the teacher's own culture and values: some may exclude the language of the child's real world because it is unreal to them; others because it is all too real – a failure of imagination on the one hand, of nerve on the other. Whatever the reasons for the exclusion, however, the consequences for the school are plain. Perhaps we no longer have unsullied spinsters lecturing uninhibited adolescents but we still have anxious and cautious suburban values. We have nurtured and cherished the autonomy of the school for long enough. Here again I must emphasize that it is not a matter of abrogating traditional responsibilities towards those in our care, but of sifting them so as to distinguish the trivial from the fundamental. The idea of the school as a place safely insulated from the outside world is no longer helpful, though it is certainly persistent – particularly in girls' schools where there is an enduring concern to prevent the girls being contaminated by the environment. Hence, not many years ago, a girl in a grammar-school class in North Lancashire was instructed: 'Gels will not talk to men in overalls!' and wondered thereafter, pardonably, how she could communicate with her Dad.

The consequences for the child are no more happy than for the school. There are schools where each utterance by the child is an act of self-exposure. At first, when he's only five, and they go easy on him anyway, he doesn't realize what is happening, but the cumulative effect of increasingly explicit disapproval soon begins to tell. He offers less and by the time he has assimilated the even greater alienness of the secondary school the teachers stand a good chance of rendering him virtually inarticulate for the purposes of school-learning. The means for this have been pioneered in schools famous for their academic standards:

BOY: When I was . . .
TEACHER: Say SIR when you speak to a member of staff.
BOY: Sir, . . . I was at . . .
TEACHER: And take your hands out of your pockets. I don't speak to the Headmaster with my hands in my pockets . . .

BOY: Sorry –

TEACHER: . . . or leaning on a radiator.

BOY: Sorry – Sorry, SIR . . . when I was at Blacton . . .

TEACHER: Well, boy, get on with it – when you were at Blacton . . . ?

BOY: Yes, Sir, when I was at Blacton Primary School . . . we used to go bird-watching on the cliffs and . . .

TEACHER: Jones, I suppose you realize what this lesson is . . . ?

Surprisingly, a rather similar situation (a lesson in which accent is being discussed) figures in a film made by the National Union of Teachers intended, ironically enough, to promote recruitment at secondary level. The film also shows a head-master entering a room where the class are 'discussing' a story by Doris Lessing and congratulating the teacher because it was so quiet that he didn't realize there was a lesson going on. It may have been a light-hearted bit of dialogue, but it is with a heavy heart that one recognizes that one may still conduct lessons that deaden all response and be praised for it!

The conclusion from all this is simply that it does not take long to reduce children to silence or to a subversive retreat into their own language. If interruption and sarcasm are not enough, the major weapon – disapproval of the child's own language – will complete the job, for this effectively undermines his confidence, and shows that you don't much care for him, his home, his friends nor anything that is his. The teachers employing such methods might do well to remember Bacon's warning: 'he that hath a satirical vein, as he maketh others afraid of his wit, so he had need be afraid of others' memory'.

Some people may assert that the dialogue is an outdated parody, that I have underestimated the place of *standards* in school, that I've said nothing about new developments that seek explicitly to make education real or 'relevant' to the child. The first point may be dealt with quite briefly. Many teachers still have a blinkered view of what is relevant to a lesson and though the pedagogic pose may nowadays be less extreme, kids are still often dominated, perhaps more subtly, by the teacher's language, as we shall see when we look at some of the research evidence in chapter two. It may be true that few teachers talk like the master quoted – as far as I can tell, this particular style is now largely confined in state schools to teachers with minor personality disorders. But even in 1973 you can easily obtain this treatment for your child – if you are prepared to pay for it. The current list of instructions for pupils at a 'crammer' includes in the section dealing with dining arrangements the following incitement to spontaneity:

If you don't like anything, don't say so as it will make you unpopular and you'll have to eat it anyway.

Even those who can't take this good, crisp, manly stuff, may still feel that the school has a responsibility to maintain standards. Some would argue that these are less undermined by traditional methods than by modern, 'permissive', ones. This is an issue to be discussed later. At this point all I shall consider is the nature and source of these standards *as they relate to speech*. In some schools, particularly in the USA, strict censorship of reading material is sometimes justified as a way of maintaining a proper respect for great literature. The position over speech is similar. There is still a preoccupation with something called 'correct speech' which is vaguely believed to resemble that of the typical BBC announcer and to differ markedly from the speech of most men in overalls. When the BBC complicates a straightforward matter by using some announcers who sound like some men in overalls, it is not surprising that there are protests. The voice of protest is often confused, however; when people talk about standards in speech it is often hard to know whether they're talking about the words they choose, about the way the words are pronounced or about the way they are strung together. Despite this, the notion of correctness may still retain some meaning for the layman. What is certain, however, is that it is altogether too crude a concept to be useful in the hands of a teacher; it is more likely to be actively harmful. When teachers become emotional about their responsibility to maintain standards of speech we may suspect that for them linguistic table-manners have become invested with moral sanctions and overtones. While one may have some sympathy with them as victims of a conditioning process, one must nevertheless assert categorically that a properly professional sense of responsibility leaves no room for continuing ignorance. On the contrary, it must demand that the teacher know something both of the way language works – and here the prescriptive concept of correctness long since abandoned by linguists will be no help to him – and of the way children learn – and here again an obsession with standards will be not merely unhelpful but positively noxious.

The third count upon which I may be accused of unfairness is the more substantial argument that so far I appear to have discounted recent developments in school organization and curriculum that have been promoted specifically to deal with some of the problems and inadequacies mentioned. Though I must leave their detailed consideration to a later chapter, let me at once acknowledge that some progress has been made. Particularly notable is a new emphasis upon the *atmosphere* of a school or classroom, an atmosphere which is conducive to initiative, curiosity and active participation – in short, to the best kinds of learning – and which depends on novel conceptions of the teacher's role and of his relations with children. The principles behind this are not new, but the scale on which they are now being applied is. There is also a new level of interaction between the school and surrounding community. This is seen not only in the work of the kind described by Michael Young and Patrick McGeeney in *Learning Begins at Home* but also in the way aspects of the environment have become bases of the curriculum and in courses where the adolescent renders service to the local community.

While progress has been made, some of the advances are more apparent than real. The subject known as 'Oral English' is a case in point. This now figures prominently in the CSE examination, with predictable effects – it is now taken seriously in some schools. It is a sad fact that in order to establish a new 'subject' in the curriculum, the quickest means is to examine it. We would be optimists if we concluded that people now recognized the importance of kids talking – it may merely mean that teachers now allow children to talk once a week, for forty minutes – one at a time, of course. Certainly a study of the examination syllabuses will show how superficial is the agreement, how restricted and unimaginative the situations in which talk is to be assessed. And when one looks more closely at the tone of official pronouncements one finds that things haven't changed much at all – listen to the 1966 *Schools Council Examination Bulletin No. 11* relating the concensus of the Steering Committee:

they recognize that the language of the coffee bar is not appropriate to school.... Any idea of examiners deliberately coming down to the lowest teenage level was rejected although the problem of contact was recognized (Barnes, Britton, Rosen and the LATE, 1971, p. 145).

In this, what one must deplore is not the idea of different 'registers', appropriate to different situations, but the tone of superiority implicit in the phrase 'deliberately coming down to the lowest teenage level'. Could there, one wonders, be anything lower than that? It might be cynically argued that by recognizing oral English, by honouring it with an exam, even with special symbols so that it stands out in our school timetable, we have shelved the problem not solved it. For it is the characteristic delusion of many teachers in this country that if something is examined it is also being taught. Responsible teachers of English are not fooled, however, for they know the size of the problem, and they know that the tendency of their colleagues to regard it as theirs alone is so pedagogically inane, that they, like their charges, are at a loss for words.

It is time we abandoned the idea that 'it's up to the English teacher'. It isn't, it hasn't ever been, it never will be. We have thought a good deal about the functions of the school but how much attention have we paid to it as a language environment? In even the latest curriculum schemes what signs are there of language receiving the attention it deserves, what signs of a language policy emerging that would run across the whole curriculum? We remain marvellously unaware of our own language in the classroom: our conscious purposes seem to an objective observer to have little connection with our own speech behaviour and its effect on those we profess to teach. Often we are merely teaching children to play games without meaning, and it is a tribute to their basic kindness that they humour us for so many hours a week, for year after year. Just how early this process starts is suggested by James Herndon whose account turns upon the daily chanting of the Oath of Allegiance to the Stars and Stripes which hangs in the corner of every American classroom:

My older son Jay was almost four when we spent a summer in Mexico. He liked Mexico pretty well, except for the odd habit the Mexican kids had of speaking Spanish. We could see that he soon understood a lot of what they were saying and urged him, as parents will, to speak Spanish, but he always refused. Perhaps he thought it no good to encourage the Mexican kids in their stubborn ways.

A year later, in the normal course, he went to kindergarten back in the United States. He found it mildly disappointing. There were no toys, he said, and when they got to go outside to play, the teacher always went with them.

I was always asking him how things were going at school, and he was always answering, Fine. I pressed for details: What do you guys do there? One day he said, when we get there we line-up, then we go in and sit down at our place, then we get up again, then we talk to the flag.

You talk to the flag?

Uh-huh.

I could see he thought the subject closed, but I said, Well, what do you say to the flag?

He turned on the TV. How do I know? he said. They're talking to it in Spanish.

The kindergarten, it seemed, had some odd habits too. Still, you could see he wasn't bothered by it. For the kindergarten didn't require him to talk to the flag himself, or to understand what they were saying to it. All it required of him was that he stand up and look as if he knew what was going on. That wasn't hard, and it didn't take long, and so he didn't mind doing it (Herndon, 1968, pp. 192–3).

Though the setting may be un-English I do not think this is an extreme example. A survey of procedures in infant and junior school religious assemblies, for instance, would reveal a great richness of what from a child's viewpoint is pure mumbo-jumbo.* And where mumbo-jumbo characterizes much of the school language environment we are forcing the child to rely

* The head teacher of a primary school regularly began morning assembly with the prayer 'Set a watch, O Lord, upon our lips . . .' – a proceeding which effectively reinforced the guilt complexes of some infants who had been slow in learning to tell the time.

increasingly on external non-verbal signals or cues to behaviour, attention to the fact that they seem able only to mumble or to follow verbal communication. This conditioning process not only determines the sterility of much that we teach but is likely to have considerable effects upon social attitudes throughout the rest of life. It is tempting to see as one of the causes of labour–management disputes the way we have trained children *not to listen*.

There is a language of the poor, a psychology of the poor. To be impoverished is to be an internal alien, to grow up in a culture that is radically different from the one that dominates society. The poor can be analysed statistically; they can be analysed as a group. But they need a novelist as well as a sociologist if we are to see them. They need an American Dickens to record the smell and texture and quality of their lives. The cycles and trends, the massive forces, must be seen as affecting persons who *talk and think differently* (Harrington, 1963, pp. 23–4, my italics).

2 Basis for Action

This chapter is intended to provide a theoretical background against which language in schools may be evaluated. Its basic contention is that our knowledge is now sufficiently advanced for us to effect significant improvements in both teaching method and curriculum design, aspects which are discussed in subsequent chapters. This is to underestimate neither the areas of disagreement – issues of enormous complexity, such as the feasibility of describing scientifically the stages by which thinking and speaking normally develop – nor the extent of our ignorance, described recently by a leading authority on language as 'nothing short of humiliating'. Problems like the nature and extent of non-verbal thinking will undoubtedly continue to engage the attention of researchers for some time to come. If such work must remain outside the scope of this chapter, this is not merely because the findings are too complex to condense but, more particularly, because they are insufficiently complete for their educational implications to be spelt out with any measure of certainty. We may nevertheless take as our starting point the assumption that thought is heavily dependent on language. There can be little doubt that for much of the time we use words to think with, or that the amount and quality of thinking that we can achieve without words are limited. J. S. Bruner, a leading American psychologist, states:

For civilized men, sentences have a compelling power to control both thought and action.

L. S. Vygotsky, a Russian of no less eminence, states:

Thought is not merely expressed in words; it comes into existence through them.

The idea of a connection between our thinking and our speaking is of course implicit in various everyday expressions.

Consider, for example, the American use of the word 'dumb'. Most of us can probably remember scenes in films where someone, having failed in interrogation to get any sense out of a youngster, dismisses him in exasperation. 'Just a dumb kid,' he may say, conveying thereby that the kid is stupid as well as inarticulate. Such popular connections between the capacity to think and the capacity to speak may appeal to common sense. The danger is that we may go on to infer that the whole matter is straightforward, however, instead of realizing that the inferences we may *legitimately* draw from 'dumb' behaviour are tentative and complex.

Something of the complexity of the matter may appear in a question posed in two contrasting contexts. Suppose this chapter had begun – ' "Why", the reader may ask, "is language important?" ' – this would have enabled me, by a convenient literary convention, to raise a question which I *wanted to answer* in a way that allowed me to take it at its face value. The artificiality of this is evident, it being inconceivable that I should follow the opening 'question' with a statement such as, 'I can't answer that'.

The situation in which a child, or an adult, appears unable to answer a question is quite different. It will not help to label him 'inarticulate' merely because he is at a loss; we shall need more evidence before we can conclude his failure is intellectual as opposed to social or emotional in origin. This becomes clearer if we imagine that I am asked the question about the importance of language in a 'live' situation. As I attempt to reply, I shall be using words to think with, not merely to interpret other words used by the questioner, but to pose a series of my own questions – for example: Does he really want to know? Do *I* know? What kind of answer would be appropriate? Was there a hint of scepticism in his voice? His jaw jutted out when he spoke, didn't it? Even as I attempt to answer these, I shall be recalling associated ideas and experiences – of people, for instance, who have asked me this kind of question in the past – to help me interpret his question.

Nor is this all; my response will have to take account of wider issues than my knowledge and my understanding of the questioner's behaviour. Much will depend on the whole situation in which the question is put: a group discussion may demand a serious, exhaustive answer that would be inappropriate at the bar of a pub.

The main inference to be drawn from all this is that there is more to language learning than learning the language. There is clearly a strong verbal element in those thought processes by which we build up from past experiences the patterns of expectation that largely guide our behaviour in social situations, but at the same time we have been learning to respond to extraverbal cues. This includes the 'reading' of whole situations in much the same way as we 'read' people's faces or gestures during conversation. In some cases we have to learn when the language is there, so to speak, to be disregarded. This is true of certain kinds of social ritual, where the words are intended to ease the social round, to create the right ambiance, rather than to carry explicit meaning. It may in fact take the youngster some time to discover this – to learn that when someone for instance asks 'How are you?' he is not normally expecting a 'real' answer and that, if you respond in full hypochondriac detail, he will probably not even hear what you say. In this connection, one American authority has stressed knowledge of when to speak and when not, what to talk about and with whom, as a vital element in linguistic competence (Hymes, 1968).

The seriousness of the kind of mumbo-jumbo in classroom or school assembly that was described in the last chapter is that what appears to the child as its ritual quality – its relative meaninglessness – was unintentional, showing that the teacher had badly misread the child's predicament. There is a limit to the amount of verbal mystification that he can endure if his willingness to learn is not to suffer. Every experience which leads him to conclude that the teacher is 'talking in Spanish' is in effect teaching him when listening is unnecesary and is imposing a restriction upon the range of situations in which he will be willing to *trust words*. Such a trust is a prerequisite of effective learning in school; the damage caused by a teacher's incomprehensibility is to be measured not in terms of particular meaning lost, but of the cumulative effect of such experiences on the child's attitude to learning. The real danger is that we may so condition him that he learns to *accept his incomprehension*.

To examine the contexts in which speech occurs, and to interpret speech behaviour in the light of particular social situations is to clarify not merely processes of socialization but, more specifically, the educational potential of different language environments. The extent to which language in school can be a vehicle for valued ways of thinking will depend on factors more varied than those to which the school customarily attends. Whatever gaps there are in it, our knowledge of the way language works in society is sufficient to locate at least some of the inadequacies and misconceptions of our school procedures, and to provide a basis for some significant reforms.

What follows – hardly more than a sample of the evidence available – will concentrate on three respects in which the schools' traditional conception of language appears inadequate. The first of these has to do with general and particular social constraints on language use and development. This will involve differentiating between major features of social background, subcultural restrictions on language development, and the particular effects of situations in school upon the child's ability or willingness to use language. Often the problems facing us will appear to result from the interaction between general and specific restrictions; the child handicapped under the former kind being particularly vulnerable to the latter.

Secondly, there is the tendency to misunderstand the relation between experience and articulation within the learning process. Remediation has sometimes been conceived as the supplying of some of the experiences that the deprived child has missed. Such approaches, though they often implicitly devalue the experiences that the child *has* had, undoubtedly have some value. The child's prime need, however, is for 'compensation' which provides not merely experiences, but situations in which he is led to use language to make experience meaningful; experience expressed being experience possessed. Only by articulating can he improve his articulation and, as he does so, gain the insight and the motivation that make further learning increasingly possible. Through language he makes the present comprehensible, the past available, the future conceivable.*

*One reason why this profoundly affects later attitudes to learning is suggested by James Britton, 'The child who puts into words what he

Thirdly – as has already been implied – the conception of language that is cherished in many schools is far too *narrow*. The concentration has been almost exclusively upon its cognitive functions in helping the child to explore the environment, indulge his intellectual curiosity and try out ideas. While it is true that the linguistic process by which the child moves from the naming of objects towards their more general and more abstract classification is fundamental to much 'school work', an exclusive emphasis on such language functions will be self-defeating except in the case of those advantaged children who have learnt at home to participate in activities which resemble those of the school. Even for them there will be a loss. As Professor Halliday has argued:

Our conception of language, if it is to be adequate for meeting the needs of the child, will need to be exhaustive. . . .
For the child, all language is doing something, in other words it has meaning. It has meaning in a very broad sense, including here a range of functions which the adult does not normally think of as meaningful. . . .
A minimum requirement for an educationally relevant approach to language is that it takes account of the child's own linguistic experience, defining this experience in terms of its richest potential and noting where there may be gaps, with certain children, which could be educationally and developmentally harmful. This is one component. The other component of relevance is the relevance to the experiences that the child will have later on: to the linguistic demands that society will eventually make of him, and, in the intermediate stage, to the demands on language which the school is going to make and which he must meet if he is going to succeed in the classroom (Halliday, 1969, pp. 34–6).

Finally, I must emphasize that the evidence to be considered does more than show up inadequacies in school procedures. It can substantially support the hitherto largely intuitive procedures of many gifted teachers whose work has been attracting more attention but who have often been diffident in its defence. The evidence, to which we now turn, not only offers them support but makes possible a clearer and more vigorous exposition

---

is doing and what he is going to do increases his persistence and is better able to carry out his plan. . . .' (1967, p. 12).

of their method. They have *guessed*, have *felt*, that language was the cornerstone of the whole educational process. We can go further than guessing.

Probably no single research illustrates the themes that are central to my argument better than that of the Russian, A. R. Luria. His book, *Speech and the Development of Mental Processes in the Child* (1959), written in conjunction with F. Ia. Yudovich, leans more heavily upon the influence of environmental and social factors on intellectual development than many western psychologists might find acceptable, but is concise, provocative and exceptionally readable.

A pair of identical twins showed a retardation in speech that was a common feature in such situations; such retardation, caused by social rather than organic (e.g. brain damage) causes, makes Luria's study more relevant to our purposes than many other accounts of the development of thought and speech in children suffering from intellectual or physical malfunction. Luria explains his interest in the twins:

Since their lives are linked in the closest way, and they understand each other in the course of joint practical activity, twins are not faced with an objective necessity for transition to speech communication so frequently as other children. . . . Speech retardation implies that a child who is relatively mature in his physical development does not possess a developed speech system. The peculiar way of life paired together with a brother (the 'twin situation'), which does not create any pressing objective necessity for speech communication, fixes this retardation. Consequently there must also be under-development of all those aspects of mental activity which depend on the acquisition of full-value speech (Luria and Yudovich, 1959, p. 37).

The subjects of the investigation, Yura and Liosha, were the last children of a large family, and at the age of two and a half had only learned to say Mamma and Papa. At the age of five their stock of words was extremely small and some were comprehensible only to themselves. Their understanding of other people's speech was clearly limited and generally only understood when it directly refered to them. They showed the capacity to communicate with each other both non-verbally and by a private language that often characterizes the life of twins brought up together, but which they possessed to an unusual degree, so that they were largely cut off and content to be. While at home, being usually left on their own, they spent most of their time playing with each other, never hearing books read nor being told stories. Despite all this the twins did not show obvious retardation. They were 'good, cheerful, energetic, mischievous, friendly and affectionate'.

The authors go on to describe the twins when they were placed in a kindergarten, noting especially their behaviour before and after their crucial separation into different classes. At first, while their behaviour was studied – and to allow a reasonable settling-in period – they were put in the same class. Here the significant symptoms of retardation appeared chiefly in the way they played. While much of their other behaviour was apparently thoroughly normal, their play was extremely limited and monotonous – even 'primitive'. Building materials, for example, were not used for building – indeed for nothing creative and meaningful – but merely for carrying to and fro, or for laying out in rows on the ground. The whole account of their play is fascinating in its revelation of the extensive repercussions that, the authors argue, follow directly from retarded speech development.

After the settling-in period, in order to 'create an objective necessity for using language in the company of speaking children', the twins were separated. The results were quickly seen. Indeed the new developments in the twins' speech were as wide-ranging as they were rapid:

Primitive speech, interlocked with practical activity, very quickly fell into the background and in the new situation the children were soon in a position to pass on to communicating with the aid of a normal language system.

Three months after the experiment began we could already observe substantial improvements in the twins' speech ... (which) ... fulfilled new functions which had formerly been absent; in place of speech interlocked with direct activity, or expressive speech, there developed narrative and then planning speech (p. 106).

The account shows how speech development may be speeded up under favourable environmental conditions and argues that the one changed factor – the acquisition of a language system – leads to significant changes in the twins' mental life:

Once they acquired an objective language system, the children were able to formulate the aims of their activity verbally and after only three months we observed the beginnings of meaningful play; there arose the possibility of productive constructive activity in the light of formulated aims, and to an important degree there were separated out a series of intellectual operations which shortly before this were only in an embryonic state (p. 107).

It is significant that the studies of identical twins have figured largely in what has come to be known as the nature–nurture debate. It may be that in emphasizing the effect of the environment upon the child's intellectual and linguistic development, Luria evades the possibility that a child may become articulate but remain stupid. For our purposes the matter is largely academic, however; the essential point is that speech development makes possible intellectual operations of increasing complexity. Whether such development, in fact, occurs must depend partly upon other factors which are less important to us merely because they are outside our control. We cannot, as yet, alter genetic endowment, but we can to a considerable extent manipulate the environments in which we expect learning to take place.

Language Learning in the Family

While Luria's work has considerably advanced our understanding of the role of language in intellectual development, it is remarkable also for a consistent emphasis upon the social settings in which such development takes place. The acceleration desired in the twins' speech development was seen to depend upon a change in their social situation; the original situation did not *demand* speech and therefore it did not come. Here Luria is following Vygotsky – 'the child's intellectual growth is contingent on his mastering the social means of thought, that is, language'. Vygotsky's definition of thought as 'inner speech' is particularly helpful; in this process the speaker is conceived as speaking *for himself,* as opposed to 'external speech', where he is speaking for others. Clearly there are many situations where the one kind runs into the other, as dictated partly by the difficulty of the subject matter and partly by the speaker's attitude to his audience. In a real sense, however, the thinking as well as the speaking may be thought of as *social*.* Both are dependent upon an audience.

Luria and Vygotsky have drawn our attention to the prime importance of child–adult interaction during the formative years. Vygotsky, according to Luria, 'arrived at the fundamental conclusion that human mental development has its source in the verbal communication between child and adult'.

Probably the feature of child–adult verbal interaction which has aroused most interest amongst researchers has been the questions children ask, and it seems reasonably established that 'middle-class' children ask more questions. Various explanations of this seem possible: in the first place their questions are more likely to be answered but this in itself reflects a life-style or home climate in which questions are common currency. The children in such homes will themselves be asked questions, will hear others asking them and will be made gradually aware that the whole universe is a mine of questions – is there to be found out about. Such an interpretation is supported by Professor Bernstein's finding that middle-class mothers were more apt to regard play and toys as means by which children find out about things.

A family's life-style may also be particularly evident in habits at meal times. Whether, for example, the family have breakfast together, during which a general conversation takes place, as opposed to one of those running-buffet situations in which it's every man for himself, has been shown to have an effect upon linguistic and intellectual development. Some sociologists have even gone so far as to assert that meal times for some families provide a situation in which conversation of an explicitly educational kind (e.g. discussing events at school, or homework)

---

*Vygotsky's view differs markedly from that first put forward by the Swiss psychologist, Piaget, whose name is associated with an emphasis upon the egocentric nature of early speech. In fact, Piaget later changed his position to meet Vygotsky, but in view of the widespread dissemination of Piagetian – or pseudo-Piagetian – thought in teacher training, the differences may be important. On this matter see Britton (1970, p. 59); Lawton (1968, p. 40); McCarthy (1954, p. 568).

takes place, whereas in other kinds of family conversation may largely consist of abuse, or assigning chores. The important thing here is not, however, explicit reference to educational topics but rather the fact that in some families the range of talk is extremely wide (and can include homework) whereas in others both the topics and the contexts where linguistic interchange takes place are restricted.

While one naturally thinks of the conversations between the child and his parents as being the crucial ones, any adult in the household has some effect. The presence of grandparents for instance has in a Negro culture been shown to relate to clearly superior linguistic and intellectual performance. One may speculate that grandparents are distinguished from other adults in these households by their being less occupied and their having in consequence, *time to listen to the child,* as well as to talk to him. This prompts reflection on the growing popularity of what sociologists have infelicitously called the 'nuclear family', often living in small flats or houses and having no room for grandparents, great aunts and the like. I remember being impressed, when marking GCE essays on the topic 'Youth and age will never agree', by the proportion of candidates who *cherished* their relationship with a grandparent or person of that generation as one in which long conversations were found enjoyable by both parties. Many candidates were at pains to emphasize their ability to talk far more freely to the grandparents than to the parents.

Long before homework becomes a problem, however, or before the moody adolescent unburdens himself to a tolerant grandmother, the social background of the home has exerted its influence upon the way the child's language develops. Thus, for example, the child's tendency to use longer sentences when speaking to an adult may be actively reinforced by middle-class parents acting as 'tutors'. This idea is put forward by the American researchers Brown and Bellugi who have distinguished a regular teaching procedure in which the child's own utterance is idealized and expanded into a more model grammatical form, after which the child gradually comes to match his next utterance to the adult model:

EVE: I sit table.
EVE: I get big.
MOTHER: That's right, when you get big you can sit at the table (Brown in Bruner, 1966, p. 38).*

Quite clearly there are many aspects of speech behaviour in which – sometimes to the latter's discomfort – children copy their parents. What precisely they may be copying at any given moment is often less than clear, however. As James Britton has argued (1970), their imitation is often based on an understanding *of the social context in which the language* is used, and is therefore not merely a matter of 'verbal parroting'. More than this, various features of the child's language are not explicable in terms of mere imitation. Many writers have drawn attention to the extraordinary 'mistakes' children make – mistakes which cannot be imitations of parental speech and which linguists now account for by suggesting that children formulate and apply rules of their own which only gradually come to conform to adult language rules. 'Foots' or 'mouses' are, at a particular stage, normal child plurals yet never heard from the mouths of adults. Similarly all those past tenses the child makes by the simple addition of '-ed': 'comed' 'goed' even 'wented'! It is true that to add -s to mark the plural, or -ed to mark the past tense, reflects an imitation, but it is also clear that the child goes further than his experience warrants and makes inductive generalizations. In this the process would appear largely to depend upon analogy: thus my small daughter who coined the word 'whobody' on the analogy of any- and some-, therefore why not who-?

As Bruner remarks, 'manifestly the strangeness of an utterance is no criterion of its grammaticality at this age'. Like many psychologists and linguists, Bruner is most struck by the productive, creative or 'generative' quality of the child's grammar, beginning from the time when most of his utterances are built round two-word combinations (viz. allgone lettuce, more hot, bye-bye dirty). These, Bruner argues, are not explicable in terms of recall or delayed imitation of adult utterances but provide striking proof of inventiveness. He cites for example the record of the two-word combinations made by one child after he had

*This work is also discussed in Britton (1970, pp. 43–7).

learnt the 'trick': by the end of the first month fourteen such combinations had been noted; second month, twenty-four; third, fifty-four; fourth, eighty-nine; fifth, 350; sixth, 1400; seventh, 2500 + (Bruner, 1966, p. 35).

On the whole our adult's view of children's language has focused too much upon its surface characteristics. In this connection one may note the valuable distinction that the celebrated American linguist Chomsky has drawn between *competence* and *performance*. When a child correctly uses a past tense, Chomsky suggests, this may be only a matter of simple imitation – we would be unwise to infer that the child understands the use in question. He 'walked' is an example of a past tense to be found in the performance level of many children and it is to be carefully distinguished from, let us say, 'he "goed" for a walk'. At a superficial level, 'walked' is correct, 'goed' incorrect, yet it is the latter which we should see as evidence of effective learning. Fundamentally, Chomsky argued, 'goed' demonstrates real *competence* for the child has not heard anyone say this but has constructed a tense inflection that reveals his growing understanding of a rule. 'Walked' on the other hand, reflects normal *performance* but whether it is evidence of competence – of real understanding – we cannot tell, since we have no means of measuring it. Chomsky's account may nevertheless afford some reassurance to parents irritated by children making mistakes which they previously managed to avoid – for instance the four year old who says 'buyed' when two years earlier he said 'bought'!

We have briefly considered one aspect of language learning that has been extensively researched and yet remains full of obscurities – so that we can hardly say more than that children imitate different kinds of speech behaviour, differently, to a different degree at different stages in their development. As James Britton has put it – 'it would seem nearer to the truth to say that they imitate people's *method of going about saying things* than to say that they imitate the things said' (1970, p. 42). The ways in which a child invents and combines words as he learns his language cannot be accounted for by theories 'based solely on traditional learning mechanisms of imitation, input, storage and practice' (Tripp, 1966, p. 81).

All this, far from merely demonstrating the complexity of the whole subject of speech development, has important implications for the classroom. It seems clear that some ineffective language teaching has been based upon over-simplified theories. Any over-emphasis upon the role of imitation may tend to reinforce the teacher's natural tendency to anthropomorphism; he is encouraged to go on assuming he is there to offer models and prescriptions which will lead the child to speak in a properly adult way. Such assumptions are not tenable in the face of what we know about the *child's own* grammar. Nor can we afford to be so sure that we know what the child is attending to when we are talking: of course it may be our words (i.e. their *meaning*) as we have tended to assume, but it may also be their shape, sound, pattern or sequence. Indeed it may not be the words in themselves at all that engage the child's interest, but our actions, extra-verbal cues or even the social setting. The extent to which the child's mode of thought differs from the adult's is becoming more generally realized. The 1971 version of the child's 'kerb drill', for instance, has been simplified, as a result of the discovery that the older version was being used not to *regulate action* but as an incantation designed to ward off evil motor cars and the like.

Language and Environment: Cultural Influences

While research has been accumulating about the impact on the individual's intellectual development of his *immediate* social and verbal environment, arguments have been going on about the extent to which his thinking processes are determined by his wider social context, by the language of the country where he lives. The debate associated with the names of Whorf and Sapir is too complex to condense but we may accept the idea that a country's language tends to point the speaker's attention in certain directions; the words available to us for colours may not actually circumscribe the number of colours we can see, but we need not expect, for example, to find very many words for fishing in the language of a Sahara tribe. Andrew Wilkinson (1971, ch. 4) gives a concise account of these issues; he argues that their relevance to education lies in 'the emphasis

Whorf lays upon the way language habitually channels our thought'.*

The possibility of a national or cultural restriction on what we can conceive or say is less important for our purposes, however, than a recent derivation from the same basic idea; namely the hypothesis that a section of society or – as sociologists might prefer to say – a 'subculture' may show clear-cut variations in behaviour, preoccupations and attitudes of a kind that are reflected in the kinds of language normally used. It is not just that environmental restrictions are reflected in the language, however, but that the purposes for which that language is adapted are limited and this may impose severe limitations upon further development. This general idea, implicit in the design of several researches already referred to, is summarized in the following passage by means of a comparison between the predicaments of deaf children and those who are culturally deprived:

From what is known about verbal communication in lower-class homes, it would appear that the cognitive uses of language are severely restricted, especially in communication between adults and children. Language is primarily used to control behaviour, to express sentiments and emotions, to permit the vicarious sharing of experiences, and to keep the social machinery of the home running smoothly. These are important uses of language. Many lower-class people are more skilful in them than better-educated middle-class people. But what is lacking by comparison is the use of language to explain, to describe, to instruct, to inquire, to hypothesize, to analyse, to compare, to deduce and to test. And these are the uses that are necessary for academic success.

If this characterization of verbal communication within the lower-class home is accurate, the parallels between deaf and culturally deprived children become much clearer. The culturally deprived child may be exposed to social uses of language from which the deaf child is barred, but in this area the deaf child is able to compensate for his lack by non-verbal means of communication. With regard to the important cognitive uses of language, however, both kinds of children are seriously deprived – the deaf child because he cannot understand what is said, the lower-class child because he is not sufficiently exposed to language in its cognitive uses (Bereiter and Engelmann, 1966, pp. 31–2).

*For an extended discussion of this, see Brown (1958).

Without pushing this parallel too far, and without endorsing either the particular concept of academic success here implied or the writers' subsequent proposals for remedial action, I believe this passage usefully emphasizes the *extent* of the handicap suffered by the culturally deprived. This matter has been the particular study of the British sociologist, Basil Bernstein, who describes his approach to the 'relative backwardness of many working-class children' as 'socio-linguistic'. As this label suggests, his work pulls together various strands from linguistic and sociological research in order to explain the problem in terms of 'a culturally induced backwardness transmitted by the linguistic process (Bernstein, 1969).*

The specific theory with which Bernstein's name is primarily associated attempts to formulate fairly precise interactions between a 'deprived' home background, the kind of language learnt there, and the consequent handicap upon the individual when placed in certain social learning situations. To put it rather loosely, certain characteristic features of life in the home may impose restrictions upon the kinds of language learnt and the purposes for which it is used, restrictions which will penalize the individual in school and restrict his intellectual performance and development. The original theory described language in terms of two 'codes', 'restricted' and 'elaborated', ways of speaking thought to be distinguishable by fairly specific characteristics and by the rather different purposes to which they were adapted. The restricted code was seen as characterized by, for example, relatively simple (even incomplete) and somewhat inflexible grammatical constructions, and the elaborated code by a greater variety of sentence structure – more complex sentences joined in more varied ways.

Most of the features originally attributed to each code are confirmed by that common sense which leads us to see differences between BBC English' and 'working-class English'. Indeed, the availability of the codes to a particular speaker was first seen as largely determined by the social class to which he belonged, the middle class being significantly advantaged, how-

* For a convenient general account of Bernstein's work see Lawton (1968, ch. 5). Recent research along the same lines is reported in Brandis and Henderson (1970).

ever, in having available *whichever* code best served the needs of the moment. For maintaining social and family relationships the restricted code was appropriate – indeed it enshrined the 'communally based culture of the working class' – but any more sustained and, particularly, any more abstract or individual purposes were better fulfilled by the elaborated code. This was less available to the working class, however, because their mode of living created less need for it, and gave less practice in it.

Any formulation of the problem in terms of only two contrasted types is prone to oversimplification. Bernstein's own early exposition of his theory must have contributed to a tendency to see the codes as more distinct from each other than was originally intended. Popular preconceptions about language have used Bernstein's analysis to support the idea current ever since the *1921 Report on the Teaching of English* – that our task is to teach children a *second* language.

The pessimistic notion that one social class speaks one code misrepresents Bernstein, however, and also conflicts with linguistic evidence that children possess all the essential structures of the language by a surprisingly early age. In other words, to use Chomsky's distinction between *competence* and *performance,* the users of a restricted code are *competent*; they *have the* necessary structures. What is restricted is their *performance*. This distinction of course relates to the purely grammatical features of the child's language; it has nothing to do with the size of their vocabulary, for example. And it remains true that children *possessing the same grammatical structures can do very different things with them*. Our ground for hope is that the potential is there; everything depends on whether they encounter the situations that will draw it out – as Luria's twins did. In this connection we may note Dell Hymes's emphasis on the critical importance of the *range* of what he calls 'linguistic routines' that are made available and shaped by the child's early language experiences (1967). In these terms the particular handicap of 'grey' children is a very severe limitation in the number of language functions that they have encountered – from which follows a limited language 'repertoire'.

Another problem frequently raised in discussion of Bernstein's work has been the difficulty of supporting the codes by detailed experimental evidence. It has been convincingly argued that the original experiments and the theoretical conclusions drawn from them paid insufficient attention to the effect of situation on both the content and the style of utterance. This makes the particularly significant features of any person's speech hard to isolate. As Chomsky has argued, descriptive studies rarely give much indication of a child's language *potential*: all they can do is record his actual speech behaviour – his performance – in a given situation, and much more complex and varied observations are necessary for us to come to any firm conclusions about the nature and extent of his linguistic competence (Chomsky, 1964, pp. 34-9).

While the linguistic features of the codes are hard to establish, the precise part played by social class in language development has also proved hard to identify. A number of recent investigations into the relationship between social class (or 'socio-economic status') and such things as intelligence, school attainment and early school leaving have thrown up factors which not only distinguish between broad socio-economic groupings but also show differences *within* any one such group. Thus in the study of family habits at breakfast (referred to on p. 36) positive, conversational breakfasting was found related to superior school performance in a way that distinguished between social classes but *also* between families *within* a given class. Findings emerging from study of a large number of schoolchildren over their whole school careers have resulted in a more subtle assessment of the effect of social class. It is becoming gradually clearer that the prime relationship is not that between social class and school performance, but between school performance and *parental attitude and behaviour*.

The specific interaction between language and social class he first suggested Bernstein now sees as unfruitful – 'the connection between social class and the linguistic codes is too imprecise' (1969). The idea – which he has helped us to conceive – of broad relationships between social class and children's use of language remains important, however. Witness the following extract from the *Review of the Literature* that prefaced a recent

American study of children's language skills in the primary school:

Differences in the linguistic skills of children of diverse social-class groups have been shown to be greatest where the group differences in social-class level are most extreme. The studies have revealed significant differences between the group mean scores of the various social-class groups in such areas as: complexity of sentence structure; certain articulation skills; length of sentences and remarks; size of vocabulary (Deutsch, Maliver, Brown and Cherry, 1964).

Bernstein's original formulation, over-simplified though it may have been, has drawn attention to possible extremes, and has confirmed the handicap suffered by working-class children when their intelligence is assessed by tests which assume a certain level of language competence. Bernstein has shown that restricted code users are hampered also by linguistic equipment which emphasizes social solidarity and values generally accepted in their neighbourhood. This involves a loss in terms of individual and personal expression and doesn't call for that explicitness which is natural in families where both curiosity and individuality are prized. Through his writings, for all their complexity, the reader gains a vivid sense of the way in which language-style results from living-style and in turn determines learning-style. This remains true of his recent re-formulation of his ideas in terms of a connection between linguistic codes and what he calls 'role systems' (as opposed to social class).

Though the idea – going back to Shakespeare and beyond – that during our lifetime we play various parts is familiar enough, our thinking may still be clouded by a suspicion that there is something insincere about 'playing a part'. Relatively few people may realize the extent to which role-playing and role-switching determine both our social competence and our capacity to learn. As Bernstein puts it, '*The particular form of a social relation acts selectively upon what is said, when it is said and how it is said*.' For him, the critical social roles (those 'through which the culture is transmitted') are learned in the family, in the age or peer group, in the school and at work, but the nature and the extent of the learning differs according to class position in society. It reflects, therefore, diverse social and intellectual orientations even among children with a common potential.

One way of studying the role systems within a family, Bernstein suggests, is to refer to the principles upon which decisions are taken and the kind of interactions that go on between members of the family. Bernstein postulates two types of family – *positional* and *person-oriented*. As often in his work the distinction between the types is clarified by an example:

Imagine a situation where a child has to visit his grandfather who is unwell and the child does not like to kiss him because the grandfather has not shaved for some time. One mother says to the child before they go:

MOTHER: 'Children kiss their Grandpa.' (Positional)
CHILD: 'I don't want to – why must I kiss him always?'
MOTHER: 'He's not well – I don't want none of your nonsense.' (Positional reason: imperative)
Another mother says in the same context:
'I know you don't like kissing Grandpa, but he is unwell and he is very fond of you and it makes him very happy.' (Bernstein, 1969).

In the positional family decisions are taken according to members' formal status (father, mother, grandparent, age or sex of child).

The essence of positional appeals is that in the process of learning the rule the child is explicitly linked to others who hold a similar universal or particular status. The rule is transmitted in such a way that the child is reminded of what he shares in common with others.

In the positional family the child is not invited to discuss the situation, nor to express his own feelings because the norms are clear and exist independently of him. In families of the 'person-oriented' type, however, the range of decisions, modifications and judgements depends upon the personal (psychological) qualities of the person rather than upon formal status. Especially important among these personal qualities is the capacity, in a conversation, *to take up the position of the other*. If I am really to understand what you say, I must do more than merely listen – to some extent I must put myself in your place.

'Where control is personal,' Bernstein argues, 'whole orders of learning are made available to the child which are not there if control is positional.'

This seems particularly important; the control exerted by the first mother resembles the kind we are accustomed to in secondary schools where, again, rules are '*assigned* in a social relationship which relies upon latent power'. In some schools the positional is virtually the only mode of social control, and appeals range from 'gels will not talk to men in overalls', quoted in chapter one – snobbery masquerading as pastoral care, to those suggesting norms based on peculiarly British concepts like 'stiff upper lips' and 'playing the game'. Along with other sociologists such as B. M. Spinley (1953) and Josephine Klein (1965), Bernstein emphasizes the way modes of speech both reveal and reinforce other aspects of behaviour and attitude; the family's whole social, emotional and mental orientation is reflected in speech and determines the extent and the kinds of learning of which the child is capable. All this implies the interdependence of linguistic and social learning, an idea so vital to the understanding of situations in school as to demand further examination.

Language and Socialization

A toddler comes to the door, bringing my wife a book she lent his mother. My wife crouches and talks to him. For quite a while he stands still; he does not – cannot? – answer, he does not – cannot? – go away. Finally she asks a question to which he can say 'Yes'. So, 'Hold my hand', she says, and she walks back to his house with him. As he gets to the drive-way, he sees his mother, calls, runs over and talks to her. He's in control of his world again.

A child coming to school for the first time may find many doors before which he can only stand stock still and speechless. The situation is *beyond* him, we say. Sometimes he may have been to the door before, with his mother, but he has never projected himself into the role of encountering that situation all on his own. Sometimes he has never been near it. How does the teacher help him to say Yes? How does she find a simple enough way of relating to him – like holding a hand? How does she restore him to his sense of a world he can control?

We might use this image in a number of ways. It reminds us that at times *all* children are at a social disadvantage, and that when they go suddenly beyond the limits of their social experience, language fails them. It reminds us that school is initially a place where social and linguistic learning are indissoluble, and thus that teachers of entry classes have first to consider how best to limit the social and linguistic demands and then how to prepare children for them. It suggests perhaps that for some children simple ritual may become a half-way house to individual, 'free' behaviour.

If for the early years at least we cannot separate restricted ways of relating to people from restricted roles for language, then the initial strategy for avoiding failure in language is clear. We should expect primary/elementary teachers to begin by looking at the social learning that goes on in their classroom, at the way children learn to work in small peer groups or 'family' groups within the class, at the roles they play within the group. Even where the work appears most individual or egocentric, we should expect to look for reverberations later on in relations with other individuals and in the sense of status within the class as a group. We should equally expect the greatest failure in classrooms where infants are given only simplified and highly ritualized roles, divorced for the most part from language learning – sitting up straight at desks, listening to teacher, imitating her movements or her language, chanting tables, copying.... Whatever the place of drill and rote, it is far from central (John Dixon 'A paper to start discussion on language teaching for the disadvantaged' given at the Walsall Seminar).

Most of us, if we think back, can recall failures that were closely akin to the failure of the toddler that John Dixon describes – situations when we too had suddenly gone 'beyond the limits of (our) social experience' and where language had consequently failed us. Nor are such failures confined to our earliest years. We may recall particularly the moody, self-doubting and introspective period of our adolescence; the times when we felt peculiarly vulnerable in unfamiliar social situations. Many a blushing parent of a 'boorish' adolescent will be thoroughly aware of the problem.

Whether one is twelve or twenty, one's comfort and competence in social situations depend not only on previous experience but upon the expectations, arising from such experience, which one brings to a fresh situation. For example, if I treat my new intake of prospective English teachers, in their first session with me, to an hour's dance drama, demanding that they remove both pullovers and shoes, I am likely to arouse a good deal of anxiety or even resentment. If on the other hand I lecture to them about drama, they will be quite comfortable – this situation they know. The reaction of relatively mature students to a totally unfamiliar teaching situation is well suggested in the following description of an unstructured course, that is to say a course in which no one – not even the instructor – knew what would happen next.

The class was not prepared for such a totally unstructured approach. They did not know how to proceed. In their perplexity and frustration they demanded that the teacher play the role assigned to him by custom and tradition; that he set forth for us in authoritative language what was right and wrong, what was good and bad. Had they not come from far distances to learn from the oracle himself? Were they not fortunate? Were they not about to be initiated in the right rituals and practices by the great man himself, the founder of the movement that bears his name? The notebooks were poised for the climactic moment when the oracle would give forth, but mostly they remained untouched (Rogers, 1967).

I am not here concerned to argue the effectiveness of unstructured courses but merely to drive home the point that to be adventurous – to be in any real sense *free* in one's behaviour – one needs to be *safe*. In deprived children this need is all the more urgent. Carl Rogers, the eminent American psychotherapist from whose *On Becoming a Person* both the previous and the following quotations are taken, has argued that many of the conclusions derived from his own field have relevance in the learning situation. In particular, if we are looking for ways of eliciting what the individual has of his own to contribute, ways of making him think creatively, we need to set up conditions of what Rogers calls *psychological safety* and *psychological freedom*.

Psychological safety. This may be established by three associated processes.
1. Accepting the individual as of unconditional worth. Whenever a teacher, parent, therapist or other person with a facilitating function feels basically that this individual is of worth in his own right and in his own unfolding, no matter what his present condition or behaviour, he is fostering creativity. This attitude can probably be genuine only when the teacher, parent, etc., senses the potentialities of the

individual and thus is able to have an unconditional faith in him, no matter what his present state. . . .

2. Providing a climate in which external evaluation is absent. When we cease to form judgements of the other individual from our own locus of evaluation, we are fostering creativity. For the individual to find himself in an atmosphere where he is not being evaluated, not being measured by some external standard, is enormously freeing. Evaluation is always a threat, always creates a need for defensiveness, always means that some portion of experience must be denied to awareness. . . . But if judgements based on external standards are not being made then I can be more open to my experience, can recognize my own likings and dislikings, the nature of the materials and of my reaction to them, more sharply and more sensitively. I can begin to recognize the locus of evaluation within myself. Hence I am moving towards creativity. . . .

3. Understanding empathically. It is this which provides the ultimate in psychological safety, when added to the other two. If I say that I 'accept you', but know nothing of you, this is a shallow acceptance indeed, and you realize that it may change if I actually come to know you. But if I understand you empathically, see you and what you are feeling and doing from your point of view, enter your private world and see it as it appears to you – and still accept you – then this is safety indeed. In this climate you can permit your real self to emerge, and to express itself in varied and novel formings as it relates to the world. This is a basic fostering of creativity.

Psychological freedom

When a teacher, parent, therapist, other facilitating person permits the individual a complete freedom of symbolic expression, creativity is fostered. This permissiveness gives the individual complete freedom to think, to feel, to be, whatever is most inward within himself. It fosters the openness, and the playful and the spontaneous juggling of percepts, concepts and meanings, which is a part of creativity (Rogers, 1967, pp. 301, 357–8).

As some case studies make abundantly clear, a proportion of those who find their way into the psychiatrist's consulting-room are profoundly unlikeable characters. Thus Roger's first rule – complete acceptance – is a hard one to follow. It is perhaps even harder in the classroom where the teacher may have to attend to, and accept, a considerable number of unloved kids who have become unlovable. This is particularly hard if their frustrations are vented in aggressive behaviour. Even here, if anything is to be achieved, there has to be an underlying acceptance.

All this is relevant to the learning situations which schools provide and, more particularly, to the 'speech climate' they offer. As we shall see later some of the conditions in the classroom make it all too easy for the teacher to misread the condition of particular pupils – to confuse, for example, non-verbal with non-vocal children, whose needs and incapacities appear similar largely because when we have thirty-six others to cope with, a can't-talker looks like a won't-talker. Often the difficulty of accurate diagnosis for a teacher who is coping with too many children is aggravated by a failure to see the pupil's behaviour as a reaction to certain kinds of social situation which impose limits on his freedom to think, and consequently upon his readiness to articulate his thought. The problem may well be further complicated by some common pedagogic assumptions about the way pupils can be taught to express themselves. Take, as an example, the teacher who enjoins a faltering pupil to 'think before he speaks'. So far from achieving its object – more coherent articulation of his ideas – this injunction frequently robs him of speech altogether. The teacher may be justified in assuming that some kind of inner verbal rehearsal leads eventually to greater clarity of expression, but this can only be so if the other, social, circumstances within the classroom situation are conducive to utterance: the child must first be *free to think*. All too often, however, the classroom provides a quite different situation, in which apparently helpful instructions of the 'think-before-you-speak' type may be little more than disguised reproofs; the kindest teacher may roll his eyes towards heaven, or assume an attitude of exaggerated patience. Whatever the signal – the word, the gesture or the tone of voice – school experience rapidly enables the pupil to recognize a hint of disapproval and renders him consequently wary of exposing himself in speech. Even where no reproof is intended or detected, the pupil's knowledge that what he is going to say will probably be screened for correctness or otherwise evaluated may be sufficient to inhibit him. One has only to think of comparable situations in which one was conscious of being 'sized-up' by a new acquaintance to recognize the effect this has upon speech behaviour.

The instruction 'think-before-you-speak' once again suggests the common recognition of the part played by words in the way we think, though it also implies that the relationship is sequential – thought *preceding* speech. This idea, though it contains some truth, seems a peculiarly schoolmasterly way of looking at the relationship. Outside the classroom with its various artificial language procedures, few people would imagine that thinking and speaking are *normally* related in this way. Far from demanding that thought be rehearsed before articulation, in everyday life we frequently accept that the processes of thinking and speaking may go on side by side; 'he's thinking aloud' we say, finding the process of groping articulation perfectly acceptable. Rather similarly, public speakers and lecturers will testify to the value of 'trying ideas out' on people, the best way of thinking something through being to talk it through. As they speak, the ideas become gradually clarified and, having spoken, they know in a new way what it was they originally wanted to say. It is particularly in cases of some difficulty that we first become aware of, or rediscover, the verbal foundation of so much of our thinking. If I find myself confronted with some electrical problem, for example, being thoroughly incompetent, I feel the need to support my thinking with verbal utterance, muttering perhaps 'Now let's see . . . if I connect this wire here . . . that one . . . must go . . . there!' Such behaviour is easily observable in children, whose early play is frequently sustained by a kind of running commentary which later appears to go underground except at the critical times of difficulty when the child needs to think it through aloud.* At school, however – especially secondary school – muttering may be frowned upon and tentativeness be only slightly more tolerable than guessing.

If Rogers's ideas are illuminating when applied to the classroom, they can also throw light on situations in everyday life, as I hope the following anecdote will show.

I was drinking one evening with a friend who is engaged on the design side of a highly specialized sector of the motor indus-

*This matter is more complex than this might suggest, however, see Britton (1970, pp. 53–62).

try, and the conversation after a while turned to my own work on the relationship of language and thought, and language and social background. Something that I said about the power of words and the effect of confidence upon their use in social situations chimed exactly with his own recent experience and so, for the first time, I heard about Alan.

Alan had been engaged to make wooden patterns for some early design work on a prototype. Previously he had been a carpenter with a building firm, working mainly and rather monotonously on roofs. He moved therefore from a well-paid but unexciting employment to a small, apparently chaotic back-street works where some half dozen men cooperated in the design and construction of their new model, indeed their revolutionary model. This was a place where both manager and the errand boy found it natural to lose count of time; there was a quite extraordinary air of cooperative involvement and excitement.

Some weeks after the original conversation I was able to call in at the factory and to appreciate its distinctive atmosphere. Even in a single visit I caught the infection and I joined my friend and his colleagues in a discussion of how a steering column from an older model could be fitted into the newly designed and just welded shell of the cab. An hour or two later I heard Alan tell his own story. It was a fairly normal story up to the time he had moved jobs. His ambitions had been relatively limited and he had been satisfied but unexcited by what he was doing. Moreover he had had a very stereotyped conception of his own relation to other people, of the people themselves and a fairly poor idea of his own capacity. At the factory he now found himself in novel relationships with sensitive and enthusiastic engineers who were not at all interested in social status or convention but only with the health and progress of their 'baby'.

In forming these new relationships Alan began to speak a different language. Above all, he began very gradually to trust himself and his own perception in a new way. One day he was astonished to find himself left over a week-end with the completion of a task that far exceeded the normal scope of a 'carpenter'. He found problems in this but also excitement, for he solved one problem by taking it home with him and looking very carefully at certain design features of the cars he saw around. The rest of the team were pleased with what he had done. What to him was more remarkable, however, was that they were not surprised.

From this point on, his confidence and zest grew and he found himself learning not merely technical terms but also the language that seemed the natural accompaniment of the new relationships he now felt himself able to form. He described his amazement at being called into a discussion with the technical manager of one of our major motor companies and at finding himself able to accept his situation without discomfort and indeed with a certain excitement. At the end of the year he had reached a point where he enjoyed discussing topics like Vance Packard's book *The Hidden Persuaders* with the firm's design manager.

It is not, I think, hard to interpret this story in terms of psychological freedom and psychological safety. It also bears out the contention of several researchers who have followed up Bernstein's work, that ability to use elaborated code is latent in apparently restricted speakers and *can be brought out in situations which encourage or demand it.* People who object to anecdotes may argue that this one proves nothing, but I remain convinced that the problems that faced Alan are common. Many of the difficulties in industry at shop-floor level – classic problems of communication between labour and management – may be seen as the fruit of seeds sown in school, where, unwittingly, we have trained people *not to listen,* to attend only to extra-verbal cues and to interpret behaviour of those around them according to stereotypes. The cumulative effect of situations in which we find it difficult to understand what is being said is that we make less effort and we find it progressively harder still to admit our failure.

Language and Learning in School

Any child may be expected to suffer from social exposure when he starts school. Many kids, for example, will be desperately conscious of wearing the 'wrong' uniform, incomplete uniform or even the new uniform which at home seemed so splendid a symbol of new status, but which at school seems indecently pristine, lacking the rents which mark out the seasoned campaigner. All this is bad enough, but the lot of the severely deprived child is far worse: set apart by more than the uniform or lack of it, he may be said to come to school wearing *the wrong mind*.

Such children will experience difficulty in learning to read, in extending their vocabulary, and in learning to use a wide range of formal possibilities for the organization of verbal meaning; their reading and writing will be slow and will tend to be associated with a concrete activity-dominated context; their powers of verbal comprehension will be limited; grammar and syntax will pass them by; the prepositions they use will suffer from a large measure of dislocation; their verbal planning function will be restricted; their thinking will tend to be rigid – the number of new relationships available to them will be limited (Bernstein, 1961).

It has already been implied that teaching as well as learning begins at home. In this connection the predicament of the disadvantaged child is illustrated by the work of Robert D. Hess and Virgina C. Shipman who conducted an experiment in which middle- and lower-class mothers were required to teach their children certain things. Part of their report demands extended quotation:

Analysis of maternal teaching styles
These differences among the status groups and among mothers within the groups appear in slightly different form in the teaching sessions in which the mothers and children engaged. There were large differences among the status groups in the ability of the mothers to teach and the children to learn. This is illustrated by the performance scores on the sorting tasks.

Let us describe the interaction between the mother and child in one of the structured teaching situations. The wide range of individual differences in linguistic and interactional styles of these mothers may be illustrated by excerpts from recordings. The task of the mother is to teach the child how to group or sort a small number of toys.

The first mother outlines the task for the child, gives sufficient help and explanation to permit the child to proceed on her own. She says:

'All right, Susan, this board is the place where we put the little toys; first of all you're supposed to learn how to place them according to color. Can you do that? The things that are all the same color you put in one section; in the second section you put another group of colors, and in the third section you put the last group of colors. Can you do that? Or would you like to see me do it first?'

Child: 'I want to do it.'

This mother has given explicit information about the task and what is expected of the child; she has offered support and help of various kinds; and she has made it clear that she impelled the child to perform.

A second mother's style offers less clarity and precision. She says in introducing the same task:

'Now, I'll take them all off the board; now you put them all back on the board. What are these?'

Child: 'A truck.'

'All right, just put them right here; put the other one right here; all right put the other one there.'

This mother must rely more on non-verbal communication in her commands; she does not define the task for the child; the child is not provided with ideas or information that she can grasp in attempting to solve the problem; neither is she told what to expect or what the task is, even in general terms.

A third mother is even less explicit. She introduces the task as follows:

'I've got some chairs and cars, do you want to play the game?' Child does not respond. Mother continues: 'OK, what's this?'

CHILD: 'A wagon?'

MOTHER: 'Hm?'

CHILD: 'A wagon?'

MOTHER: 'This is not a wagon. What's this?'

The conversation continues with this sort of exchange for several pages. Here again, the child is not provided with the essential information he needs to solve or to understand the problem. There is clearly some impelling on the part of the mother for the child to perform, but the child has not been told what he is to do. There were marked social-class differences in the ability of the children to learn from their mothers in the teaching sessions.

Each teaching session was concluded with an assessment by a staff member of the extent to which the child had learned the concepts taught by the mother. His achievement was scored in two ways: first, the ability to correctly place or sort the objects and, second, the ability to verbalize the principle on which the sorting or grouping was made.

Children from middle-class homes were well above children from working-class homes in performance on these sorting tasks, particularly in offering verbal explanations as to the basis for making the sort.... Over 60 per cent of middle-class children placed the objects correctly on all tasks; the performance of working-class children ranged as low as 29 per cent correct. Approximately 40 per cent of these middle-class children who were successful were able to verbalize the sorting principle; working-class children were less able to explain the sorting principle, ranging downward from the middle-class level to one task on which no child was able to verbalize correctly the basis of his sorting behaviour. These differences clearly paralleled the relative abilities and teaching skills of the mothers from differing social-status groups (Hess and Shipman, 1965).

Without assuming that a British replication of this experiment would yield the same results, such evidence fits in with the picture that has been emerging of what we might almost call subcultural predestination. Certainly Bernstein felt confident enough about the effects of home background upon the language and learning of working-class children to make the very specific predictions quoted earlier. From the earliest days we may expect the 'linguistic distance' between the disadvantaged child and his teacher to be considerable. More serious still, the evidence suggests that it will grow.

In part this may indicate the cumulative effect of some teachers' language strategies, which exacerbate a handicap that is already severe. We may also note that it is in the early years that the teacher learns what to expect of a pupil. A number of studies have revealed a close connection between teacher expectation and pupil performance (for example, Douglas, 1964; Rosenthal and Jacobson, 1968). The child whom everyone calls a 'dud' will soon begin to behave like one, indeed to believe that he *is* one; conversely, the performance of children whom teachers mistakenly believe to be bright has been shown to improve. One may speculate that both the actual language strategies the teachers use and the less explicit ways they tend to type-cast pupils lie behind evidence such as the following:

Receptive language and social-class differences
Social-class differences in certain receptive language skills are considerably more apparent at fifth grade (age ten to eleven) than first

grade (age five to six). At first-grade level, middle-class children gave significantly more meaningful responses to the teachers' speech items than the lower-class subjects did. At the fifth grade, lower-class children did less well than their middle-class peers.... They less often replaced the exact missing word, less often filled the deletion with a contextually meaningful response and less often were able to substitute for the deleted word a word correct in grammatical form. ... The data support the point of view that there is a language barrier between the middle-class teacher and the lower-class child, particularly the child in the higher elementary school grades. This is consistent with data showing that IQ differences due to social-class increase with age (Deutsch, Maliver, Brown and Cherry, 1964, p. 123).

In all probability the problems are most obvious at secondary level. Here Douglas Barnes's study of language used by teachers in twelve lessons with children in their first term of secondary school is particularly suggestive. Barnes describes his study as

a preliminary investigation of the interaction between the linguistic expectations (drawn from home and primary school experience) brought by pupils to their secondary school and the linguistic demands set up (implicitly or explicitly) by the teachers in the classroom.

He was interested in the teachers' questions, the amount of pupil participation, the extent to which the teacher used a special subject vocabulary, the relationship of teacher and pupil, and whether language was used for tasks that might have been better done by other means. In particular, by analysing the questions used by teachers in five lessons, Barnes sought to clarify:

the teachers' covert interpretation of the nature of what they were teaching – that is the interpretation *that they were acing upon* whatever they may have told themselves about the purpose of the lesson. And this covert version of their subject is important because it will be 'learnt' by the pupils *as part of the role of being a learner in that* subject (Barnes, Britton, Rosen and the LATE, 1971, p. 22).

This idea is of extreme importance. Barnes is pointing out that a geography teacher, for example, is mistaken if he equates what he is teaching with what the children are learning. While they are probably taking in a proportion of the explicit subject matter, they are also learning (amongst other things) what it means to learn geography, as taught by Mr X. To be even more specific, they are learning what is needed to pass time comfortably in that situation; as in most other situations at this stage of their school career, they will be particularly anxious to know 'what is expected of them'. Clues to follow in their behaviour take precedence over any thirst they may have for geographical knowledge. In this connection Bernstein's suggestions about the relationship between kinds of learning and modes of social control seem particularly relevant; they go some way towards explaining why so many teachers find so many children *dim*. Their plight is evoked by Barnes:

An enormous amount of talk washes over pupils in lessons.* Their problem must be to select from it those utterances which make explicit the criteria by which their performances will be judged. Some teachers mark these utterances with different intonation patterns and vocal quality. When teachers do not do this, pupils must be faced with a difficult problem of selective attentiveness. It seems that some children so largely fail to perceive the nature of the given tasks that they are in effect not solving problems but copying external models (Barnes, Britton, Rosen and the LATE, 1971, p. 37).

One has only to follow a class of children through a series of lessons taken by different subject specialists to see how much they have to learn in terms of social behaviour. The observer will notice that Form 1A going into Room G is – even after only a few weeks' conditioning – a different class from the 1A which went to Room 8 some forty minutes earlier; already a whole set of language and social expectations have been associated with particular subjects, particular furniture, particular teachers. With experience children become expert in reading the signs of the environment: one of my colleagues recounts how he *knew* that maths lessons would be more than usually uncomfortable on those days when the teacher wore a blue suit.

*Just how much has been discovered by techniques of 'interaction analysis' used in the USA by N. A. Flanders. His 'law of two thirds' relates to the proportion of lesson time given to teachers' talk. Work along similar lines in this country reinforces his evidence (see E. C. Wragg, unpublished doctoral thesis, University of Exeter).

Similarly, I recall a classics master who rarely wasted his important questions simply because he always removed his glasses before posing them.

It must be emphasized that such problems as that of selective attentiveness are faced by all children in school, not merely by those who are already linguistically deprived. Too often teachers seem unaware of both the nature and the range of the learning that takes place under their very noses, just as they may never have realized that the questions they ask are not really questions at all. Every winter term, for example, teachers may be heard to complain of the poor quality of this year's Lower Sixth. This may be found particularly puzzling in the light of the same pupils' excellent performance in the fifth form during the previous year. It should not be, however. At a time when they are already preoccupied with the strains and excitements of adolescence, they have moved into a situation where the teachers' expectations are quite different from anything they have known before. Last year they had to be good sponges; now they are expected to have minds of their own. The strain of the adaptation, in itself similar to the transition from primary to secondary school, often shows in the stodginess, the *dumbness,* of which teachers complain.

If problems of this kind confront all children, it is clear that some are peculiarly unequipped to meet them. For those whose social and linguistic experience is severely restricted, what for us is a normal enough teaching situation becomes little short of a social survival test. It is ironic that some teachers should have given so much thought to remedying kids' lamentable 'cockiness' and to 'taking them down a peg'. What appears as cockiness is often a defensive stance which some pupils adopt in face of an inexplicable or threatening situation, while others may merely retreat into their own private world. Just how lost children may be in a classroom emerges sometimes from professional observations:

the writers have found culturally deprived children to be strangely indifferent to the content of verbal utterances while being acutely concerned with the effect that their utterances have on other people. A question that begins with 'Can you tell' – or 'Do you know' is invariably answered 'Yes', often before it is completed. These beginnings are evidently recognized as signals that 'Yes' is the desired answer. Yes – No questions have to be used with great circumspection in the teaching of these children because the children are so adept at and intent upon 'reading' the teacher's expressions and inflections for clues to the desired response. The children may even succeed in giving correct answers without fully understanding what *yes* and *no* mean (Bereiter and Engelmann, 1966, p. 37).

Observations like this emphasize yet again the need for more talk in school – but of what kind? The conventional teacher-directed 'discussion periods' are inadequate, providing situations in which the emphasis is all too easily switched to trying out *people* as opposed to the trying out of ideas, and the practice in articulating them, which were the original aims. Other reasons for dissatisfaction are suggested in Sidney Bolt's *The Right Response*:

There are certain topics on which most students have something to say, namely the burning questions of the hour, such as death on the roads, and the ethics of pre-marital sexual intercourse. Unfortunately, discussion of such topics does not develop the use of language. They fall well within the scope of a rudimentary language. The newspapers and television have seen to that. The rudimentary language merely borrows clichés from the literate one, as the language of the kitchen borrows phrases from French. Nothing could be more stereotyped than private discussion of a publicized question. . . .

Public issues are inevitably battlefields, with opposing forces ranged against each other, and people who are sufficiently interested to discuss them will have already joined one side or the other. Discussion between such people therefore takes the form of warfare, an activity in which, as Henry V pointed out at Harfleur, it does not pay to be sensitive and flexible. Sensitivity and flexibility are, however, the very qualities the English teacher aims at fostering (1966, p. 31).

Bolt is concerned to argue the special importance of literature, contending that the essential 'sense of involvement can only be produced by presenting the student with something particular, an individual exhibit rather than a wide issue, and asking him what he makes of it'. While his argument is generally close to the view of literature implied in chapter four, it does not emphasize the very special difficulties that discussion periods of the type he effectively criticizes present to the *disadvantaged* pupil whose language may be too rudimentary, or his self-confidence insufficient, for him even to borrow clichés from the literate language in the way Bolt suggests. Discussion periods of public issues *appear* effective only in those settings where the pupils are advantaged in having parents who customarily and coherently discuss such matters and whose opinions can therefore be used as models. To some extent, the girls in a direct-grant school who appear able to sustain astonishingly abstract discussions of public issues are role-playing their father and mothers – they are thinking vicariously. The disadvantaged have no such resource.

Experience alone is not enough, for we hardly possess it until it is articulated. For this to happen, as Rogers's testimony suggested, the pupil needs to feel comfortable in a way rarely possible in a formal classroom where the presence of the teacher, to say nothing of thirty-five other pupils, imposes social constraints which inhibit precisely the kinds of talk that are needed. A brief extract from the tape of a student's discussion with a remedial class of fourteen year olds, suggests some of the effects upon utterance of a deprivation that is both linguistic and social:

STEPHEN: I like the last day of the week 'cos it's the very last you see.
JONATHAN: Because there's games – see.
STEPHEN: No, I don't like games.
STUDENT: Do you think that teachers are very unfair?
STEPHEN: Some of them is – that ratbag at the top in room X is a proper shit.
JONATHAN: Oh yes.

Experienced observers of deprived children have often drawn attention to the fact that they seem able only to mumble or to shout, a characteristic seen as testifying to their lack of experience in the expository uses of the language. Stephen lacks control of more than volume, however; the problem for pupils like him is not merely a matter of saying something more or less loudly, but also of saying more or less *than they mean*. Apparent frankness, like that quoted, might be called 'semantic shouting' and this tends to alternate with unintentional understatement, 'sempanic whispering'. The difficulty for Stephen and his friends arises not only from their lack of synonyms, and poor control of nuance, but from their peculiar social vulnerability in new situations. While I don't claim that Stephen 'didn't mean it' (I'm sure the opposite is true), the novel experience of unburdening himself, *in school, to an adult,* is certain to have affected whatever ability he had for adjusting speech to the social context. To say all this is really to provide a gloss on Bernstein's comment cited earlier (p. 45) 'The particular form of a social relation acts selectively upon what is said, when it is said and how it is said.' At a more sophisticated level, with an older class perhaps, children may resort to a frankness apparently similar to Stephen's in order to test either the teacher's authority or the sincerity of his expressed interest in their opinions.

It is significant that thinking aloud is an activity not normally encouraged by the speech climate in the classroom. This is particularly true at secondary level, where teachers may be so preoccupied with their own conception of what is to be learnt that they ignore or actively discourage other kinds of learning; there is not time to wait while pupils *grope their way towards thought.* It is probably only in the pupil-to-pupil talk of small groups that the adolescent can feel safe enough to think aloud in a way that enables him to 'realize' and recognize aspects of his experience, his emotions, his personality that he has hitherto kept private even from himself. In this context, the teacher's role may be largely confined to making such situations *feasible,* and to offering some initial stimulation – perhaps in the form of film or literary extract. After that he must withdraw, and have faith; the indifferent cook who opens the oven door every two minutes will probably find that the cakes aren't rising.* The adolescent's support must now come from his peers, though pupils who have had sufficient experience of such situations seem increasingly ready to re-admit the teacher to their discussions. In 'Talking to learn', James Britton illustrates and analyses group discussion of this type:

In talk of this kind trivialities may break in at any moment (though it is never easy to be sure what is trivial in somebody else's concern):

*It must be emphasized that all this refers to the teacher's role in *one* situation designed to foster *one* kind of language development. Clearly, other situations demand other roles in some of which much more direct intervention by the teacher will be appropriate.

it does seem, however, that as this conversation moves on it grows in its power to penetrate a topic and resist the trivial distractions. At its most coherent points it takes on the appearance of a *group effort at understanding*, and these coherent passages are more frequent in the later phases than in the earlier.... The mutually supportive roles these speakers play make it possible for them, I believe, to exert a group effort at understanding, enable them, that is, to arrive at conclusions they could not have reached alone and without that support (Barnes, Britton, Rosen and the LATE, 1971, pp. 97–8).

In order to illustrate something of the possibilities of such talk, I have included in an appendix the transcript of a conversation between four girls in a secondary modern school. This followed a BBC 'Speak' programme which raised the problem of failure, using a short story about a Welsh boy who failed the 'eleven plus'. The discussion shows how – in an unpressured, informal situation – the girls are able to explore and extend their thoughts and feelings, articulating them not merely more fully than they could have done with a teacher present, but also with an increasing sensitivity to the reactions of the listeners. They are learning about themselves and about others; and in learning and seeking the language that will do it justice.

The potential impact on learning and attitude of talk between secondary pupils is only becoming apparent. This comes about partly through the accumulating experience of the need, in unstreamed teaching situations, to depend upon children's capacity to work in small groups,* but many primary teachers, used to such situations, have long recognized the importance of talk in every part of the curriculum. In any subject, even at secondary level, there is a clear place for the 'operational' talk which extends or guides pupils' thinking as they work together in small groups. There ought also to be opportunity in more subjects than merely English for talk that is exploratory or reflective – talk wherein pupils support each other in the movement towards greater articulateness, in gaining control of themselves and of their world. The second kind is easier to understand than to provide for, however. While the aim is not the promotion of mere noise or chatter, we are still unduly sensitive to both; above

---

* Some of the possibilities are made clearer in chapter four.

all, perhaps, we have to control our obsessive, professional, fear of something we call 'irrelevance'. Despite such difficulties, many teachers are discovering the surprising fact that, given the right starting point or setting, unsupervised pupils can actually be expected to sustain thoroughly useful conversations.*

To facilitate new kinds of talk in the classroom, however, implies changes in the social climate it provides. In most subjects in the curriculum we are seeing a move away from the teacher as *instructor* towards a warmer, more informal role. As Barnes has convincingly argued, we cannot talk about relationships in the classroom without implying a great deal about the language that is used there. Barnes has emphasized above all that

the crucial quality of a teacher's language is whether it is warm, exploratory, available, encouraging the child to involve himself actively in learning, or whether it is cold, inflexible, defensive, and discouraging (Barnes, Britton, Rosen and the LATE, 1971, p. 64).

Where language has gone sour in the secondary school, this may well be the result of divorcing pastoral and academic considerations – as if caring for children and teaching them were two different things, an idea which at primary school level is eminently impractical. In many large secondary schools, however, a separation of these functions is implicit in use of the term 'teaching staff' as opposed to 'house staff'. Though administratively convenient, this appears potentially dangerous – it institutionalizes a misleading distinction.

Even when his school's organization poses no problems, however, the teacher's new, less formal role is not an easy one. What he is to do is often a good deal less clear than what he is not to do. Above all, perhaps, the new role is hard to adopt because of the way most have been conditioned; on the whole teachers are drawn from those sections of the community best able to profit from the kind of traditional language environment that schools have provided. Because they have achieved success within this system, teachers are inclined both to value it and to undervalue

*See, for example, the discussion by eleven to twelve year olds of a single poem in *Teachers' Centre Discussion Materials 1* (May 1970), Schools Council Project, *Language Development in the Primary School,* directed by Mrs C. Rosen, University of London, Goldsmiths' College.

some kinds of learning and language activity that are outside their own experience. In the old days it was much easier to distinguish between personal and professional relationships with children and it is not surprising if some new teachers – uncomfortable in their new role – make mistakes.*

This fact may be an indictment of our teacher preparation, of the pressures exerted upon the teachers by society at large, or of the conditions under which we expect the teachers to work, but the mistakes do not invalidate the theories of learning upon which the new emphasis upon relationships exists. The emphasis may be defended on humanitarian, political or religious grounds but it is not these that concern me. The point is simply that satisfactory relationships within the classroom are increasingly perceived to be a precondition of effective learning.

Some Emotional Aspects of Language Learning

With the growing understanding of the importance of relationships has come an increased recognition of emotional factors. This is a field where our own experience is little help. The general nature of cognitive learning in the classroom is fairly familiar to us – we at least remember what is meant by learning facts. The influence of emotion upon learning – the affective aspect – is much less clear, however, and the idea of positively 'educating the emotions' may convey little meaning to most people. Nevertheless one can conclude that part of this difficulty of describing learning processes lies in the infinitely varied inter-weaving of feeling and thought in any situation studied. Hence most classifications of learning processes – above all those based on a theoretical separation of the cognitive and affective strands – are very clumsy tools for the researcher. It is worth recalling Sylvia Ashton-Warner's discovery that Maori children learnt most easily the words like 'ghost', that were heavily loaded with emotion (1966). It is not just a matter of strong feelings about the subject, or about learning, however, the point to be made at the outset is that all learning – even the most boring – is *feeling-laden*.

The matter, complicated as it is, becomes clearer if we begin

*For a full and perceptive discussion of their problems see Hannam, Smyth and Stephenson (1971).

by looking at some negative indications – at situations where something has gone (emotionally) wrong and where learning has in consequence been impaired. The learning of reading shows the powerful effect of emotional factors upon developing competence. A substantial body of research evidence would now lead us, for example, to expect radical difficulties in mastering techniques for children whom we might term maladjusted (Sampson, 1966). Many poor readers are known to belong to one of two categories: they may be *aggressive* perhaps as a result of harsh disciplinary methods, unfavourable comparisons with their brothers and sisters, or marked rejection by their parents; or they may be *submissive* perhaps because they have been over-protected or because they have been thought to have bad health.

The relationship between reading and adjustment is concisely discussed in Dorothea McCarthy's classic chapter on 'Language development in children,' (1954). Among the researches she refers to is one carried out with children aged six to seven who were known to have special reading problems. Instead of remedial instruction, these children were given 'non-directive therapy' designed to make them 'feel secure in the classroom' and encourage them '*to talk out* their problems while painting or engaging in other creative work'. After three and a half months of this treatment, the results were seen in 'marked gains in all measures of reading achievement ... for nearly every child'. Since other research, using play therapy, pointed in the same direction, the implications of such studies for teaching, she concluded, were 'indeed challenging'. Scarcely less so was another experiment to which she refers; this showed that maladjustment in the *teacher* 'was definitely associated with adverse or indifferent results for the children in both reading and personality adjustment' (McCarthy, 1954, p. 610).

We do not, of course, have to look at children with marked personality disorders in order to assure ourselves of the connection between emotion and learning. Any interested parent of a child at infant school must have noted the way his performance varies weekly or monthly according to his general morale or state of mind, a state of mind that is often dependent upon incidents which to an adult seem unbelievably trivial. My own youngest, now five, after two weeks' rapturous enjoyment of being a 'big schoolgirl now', suddenly went off the whole thing for no apparent reason and it took about a week – a very uncomfortable week for all of us – to discover the cause. The school 'monitor' attached to her dinner table apparently had said some 'nasty things' to Felicity, including a phrase which particularly rankled, 'We don't want this *thing* here, do we?' Within one day of the teacher's being aware of what was happening and the monitor's being kindly and discreetly moved to another sector of responsibility, Felicity was reading happily again and only too anxious to get on with school. A trivial incident, perhaps, but a succession of such incidents may establish for a child the whole tone of a subject and may determine success or failure.

So much for the negative aspect. On the positive side enough has already been said to indicate the quality of relationships and the emotional atmosphere that facilitate learning. The place of children's talk in fostering confidence and in learning to form, develop and articulate ideas has been emphasized. The story of Alan, and Carl Rogers's concepts of psychological safety and psychological freedom are again particularly relevant. All this concerns what we might call the emotional background to learning, as opposed to the education of the emotions. The range of situations in which the teacher may make a positive impact upon the way the pupil feels will only become apparent when we look in detail at the classroom, but one or two issues may be raised at this point.

In his important book, *Language and Learning* (1970, p. 77), James Britton particularly stresses the place of expressive, play-elements in language development and refers to *The Voice of Poetry in the Conversation of Mankind* (1959), in which Michael Oakeshott expounds the idea that in our early language learning 'we are moved not by the desire to communicate but by the delight of utterance'. The range of uses to which language is put as we learn to speak it is very inadequately reproduced within the school environment and Oakeshott's emphasis on 'delight of utterance' usefully reminds us how much the efficient learning of a language depends upon our playing with it, savouring it, messing around with it. As the Opies' book, *The Lore and Language of Schoolchildren* (1959), makes clear, these are both natural and enjoyable activities.

Language play remains important long after the pre-school phase, but it is an aspect which primary schools *under present conditions* find hard to cater for adequately. It is also much less irrelevant to the purpose of secondary education than has often been assumed. This last point is illustrated by a graduate student, Miss Sheila Robinson, in an account of work done, on teaching practice, with a first-year remedial class in a rural area:

1C were astonished whenever they discovered a new way of playing with words, a less straightforward means of expression. Kerr put his hand up one day, looking proud but doubtful, and showed me what he had written: 'Have I made a joke, Miss?' He had put:

Mr Parkin's hair is like a forest,
His beard is like a bush,
His sideboards are like FURNETURE.'

She comments:
'It was not much of a pun, certainly, but to a child who had never been conscious of double-meanings and ambiguities in words that could be manipulated it seemed miraculous.'

She goes on to recount how 1C's excitement in 'discovering' similes was for many the start of poetry writing, for Colin for instance:

The Farmer
The old farmer is a hard-working man,
His clothes and hat covered in dust
The hat tatty with age
A pipe in one hand and a rotting stick in the other.

His face is ciricalled with age.
And his eyes are biger than a light bubl
His ears are like wind brakes
And his hands are like a fighters fist.

Strangely, the effects of this excitement lasted, so that some children tried out ideas with no prompting. This she found, sandwiched between two factual pieces:

The Cow
The Cow is big and bony
Her undercarriage swings as she dawdles
She slowly lumbers in to be milked.

The idea of English as 'fun' is easily oversimplified, becoming identified with a frivolous self-indulgence which has little to do with 'real work'. Children playing with similes, or discovering a pun in the way described may, however, be learning for perhaps the first time to perceive their own language. If the English teacher is increasingly preoccupied with expressive language functions this does not mean that he need abrogate his responsibility to promote the conscious understanding of language in use. Work like that described above shows that language play has a conceptual as well as an emotional (and motivational) aspect, fun with words involving fun with ideas. Bruner, for example, emphasizes the way words permit an

experimental alteration of the environment, without having, so to speak, to raise a finger by way of trial and error or to picture anything in the mind's eye by imagery. 'What if there were never any apples?' a four year old asked upon finishing one with gusto (Bruner, 1966, p. 37).

The new stress upon what is frequently, and loosely, called 'creative' English arises largely because personal and expressive functions of language appear neglected in the rest of the curriculum. Many English teachers believe, in the words of Suzanne Langer that:

a wide neglect of artistic education is a neglect in the education of feeling. Most people are so imbued with the idea that feeling is a formless total organic excitement in men as in animals, that the idea of educating feeling, developing its scope and quality, seems odd to them, if not absurd. It is really, I think, at the very heart of personal education (Langer, 1958).*

The English teacher's traditional faith in the usefulness of literature – as influencing feeling and as promoting understand-

*In this connection, the Schools Council Curriculum Study, *The Arts and the Adolescent*, should be noted. Its interim findings, which lay stress on 'an intelligence of feeling', suggest that the final outcome will be of major importance.

ing of both oneself and other people – would lead him to argue that the understanding gained via the feelings and the imagination is real knowledge. To quote Langer again: 'Self knowledge, insight into all phases of life and mind, springs from artistic imagination. That is the cognitive value of the arts.' In literature, as in other branches of the arts, we hope to put the pupil in a position to contemplate and understand feeling by objectifying it. In both literature and their own writing, as well as in their talk, children are exploring their world and their own identity. The extent to which we help them to realize, articulate – and, finally, refine the articulation of – their feelings about experience will determine to a considerable extent both their attitudes and their capacity to learn.

We have looked at the development of language from a number of angles in the hope that even so incomplete a survey will enable us to think about the school situation more clearly. I do not want to argue that a teacher has to be conversant with a whole body of research. The practical inference to be drawn from the outline I have given is much simpler. To be a well-equipped teacher does not necessarily mean to understand the precise *ways* in which the child's language differs from that of the adult, but to realize the *extent* of that difference, and consequently the nature and extent of the demands we make (consciously and unconsciously) upon the child. Knowledge of the subject is of course useful but imagination is equally important. James Britton has put this well:

Children have to face disappointments, it is true. 'He has to learn' is a statement that in general cannot be denied. But its application in a particular situation will be just or unjust in accordance with *our* ability to appreciate the nature of the re-construing of the *child*'s world it demands of him (1970, p. 50).

3 *Language Deprivation in School*

Primary

Eric – ESN by Brian R. L. Lee

Outside, a steely sky and plate
Of trodden two-months' snow
Cover the playground, and the fields
That reach up from the railway
And climb to the estate;
A surviving crow
Tugs at a shred of vegetation.

Inside in the warm, the other eight
Keep turning round
As if this was the way to find
And trap, one word
Of all the words that come and go,
The answer that will make the question let them go –
At times their eyes light up with what they find.

Last evening you came to me, lost
Because you had lost a shilling,
Face frozen past
Tears you had not wept:
The whole world crossed
You, till I gave you a shilling.

Today you smile your thanks simply
At the desks, the walls, the others,
Blank paper, blank snow
And teacher, who does not know
What's best for you,
Who would like to give you more shillings.

(*Use of English*, Autumn 1969.)

There are many moving accounts by teachers of deprived, desperate or disabled children but I know of no more economical evocation of their predicament than Brian Lee's poem, and no more appropriate introduction to the central concerns of this chapter. In particular it evokes the bleakness of the environment in which they often live, and of the classrooms where many of them are 'taught'. More important still, the difficulties that Eric's teacher faces, like those of Eric himself, are in no way peculiar to classes or schools for those who are, technically, 'educationally subnormal'.

Before I had completed a programme of visits to urban primary schools, often set in partially demolished slums or equally barren new estates, it had become hard not to see the children as victims of a hostile environment in which the teacher's task was insurmountable. Demolition means a shifting population: one head of a school of 350 children informed me that in *each* term of his first year sixty children had left to be replaced by sixty others. And in any case one-third of the 350 came from homes with six or more children.

Even schools with a stable population and a less uniformly deprived intake suffer from over-crowding. One infants school in a neighbouring area had a waiting-list of fifty, it being *normal* to admit children a term late. When you go out of the playground you pass a row of low buildings which in years gone by must have served to store equipment, coal, etc. The largest of these, on the end of the row, would make a very useful potting shed but it is used as a classroom from Easter to Summer each year; if it were not, fourteen children would miss another term of the education to which they are entitled and which they so sorely need.

Overcrowding is not of course peculiar to the most decayed areas – in fact the situation is often worse in the estates where people have been resettled. In any case it would be as wrong to suggest that those living in any particular architectural environment are therefore linguistically deprived as to assume that the quality of education was dependent on the school building. Both grim surroundings and poor school buildings however may conspire to impose a further strain upon the teacher. They have something else in common: each may provide a likely setting for particular kinds of deprivation.

The deprivation we associate with poor home backgrounds

is not of course something the teacher can, at any rate in the short term, remedy. He can, however, try to ensure that he does not add in-school deprivation to out-of-school deprivation. The society which sends a child from a deprived background to a deprived school to be taught by deprived teachers may justly claim to have done the worst it can for him. Even the most dedicated and capable teacher may be defeated by deficient provision. If his classroom is as bleak as the surrounding area he cannot be held solely responsible.

There is however a kind of bleakness which has less to do with physical than emotional conditions. Here the prime failure – for which the teacher *may* be responsible – is one of imagination. It is not enough to *know* that the child from a deprived area will probably have developed his language in ways that are an inadequate preparation for the linguistic demands that the school and the classroom will impose upon him. Brian Lee's poem powerfully suggests what this means to an individual child. It is not entirely feasible, of course, to expose oneself to feel as wretches feel – to put oneself, for example, in the place of an eight year old who acts as substitute mother, opens up the house after school, shops and prepares tea for the rest of the family; the middle-class mind boggles similarly at the idea of living to the same ripe old age in a city like Birmingham without knowing what a railway station is, or is like – let alone a farm. It is even harder to conceive learning to read in the face of such impoverished experience – to read correctly words which remain mysteries.

Hard though it may be, the teacher must remain imaginatively in touch with these realities. Only then will he be able to check his 'righteous indignation' over a child's inability to concentrate. Most of the worst crimes against children result less from lack of knowledge than from uncultivated imagination – I recall the headmistress of a new, architecturally advanced, open-plan school who entered a classroom and severely demanded to hear 'some of those slow readers', thus effectively undermining, in an instant, the gradual growth of confidence the class teacher, over a term, had been at pains to encourage. Rather similarly, there are classrooms where the noticeboard carries a reading graph of each child, a black line showing his progress and a red one the progress of some average or 'normal' child. This, of course, is useful if one wants to ensure that he can tell, at any moment, how subnormal he is. At the same time it harms him in ways that no linguistic expertise alone on the part of a teacher can remedy.

Finally, as it works on our imaginations, the scene Lee has evoked directs us towards some of the most important theoretical issues. In it, we see pupils operating in a school situation which is *largely meaningless to them* and which therefore forces them to resort to a frantic trial-and-error learning. This is not the special problem of an ESN child, to be answered by some dazzling remedial technology. Eric's problem is similar to that of many children in many schools. Specific remedial techniques or drills have a place, but they will only be fully effective when we have totally re-thought the place of language in every subject in school. Eric's problem may be special in degree, but not in kind. His predicament may be at one end of a continuum, but at the other is the brilliant Ph.D. student who found the jargon involved in an 'introductory' lesson on statistical method so baffling, despite her training in science, that she burst into tears.

While the child's problems are becoming more apparent, what is less easily recognized is that in an unfeasible teaching situation, the teacher as well as the child is a victim. Imagine receiving written work like this:

D cabbage as pattern e walk wolea a pattern il the ke I etin in school at Vola Iamoha af I a mon a I go tia of tia I e insa IM it Ig d tia Di tit ic d otic a the I come c the theorad cos the igine ra come klo at neigh ih the fr so the tiv.

Connie Rosen, from whose briefing paper on teacher training to the Walsall Seminar the quotation above was taken, was talking about the impact of this sort of thing upon students in training. She went on to argue that we need to have some understanding of what it means to confront someone like Egerton – let alone a class of Egertons – for the first time. To be unable to cope with such a situation because, like one's fellow students, one lacks both knowledge and experience is bad enough; to have the requisite skills and experience and yet be unable to use them is infinitely more demoralizing. I fancy that a great deal of what looks to the external observer like reactionary, unenlightened or merely ineffectual teaching has its roots in what must for a truly professional teacher be a crucifying experience: knowing how to do much better but feeling that as things stand improvement is impossible. While impotence alone is uncomfortable, caring impotence is worse. When, however, the teacher is knowledgeable as well as compassionate, impotence must be intolerable.

The nature and extent of the problems confronting him emerges from the objectivity of the following list* of personal characteristics and language habits of the disadvantaged, drawn up by one of the study groups at the Walsall Seminar in order to suggest the symptoms that the teacher should be looking for:

Personal characteristics

1. Substitutes aggressive action for aggressive language.†
2. (a) Generally poor physical coordination.
   (b) Handwriting exhibits poor physical control.
3. Aimless activity.
4. Persists in parallel play (cf. ref. to Luria p. 34).
5. (a) Upset by broken routine.
   (b) Holds desperately to the familiar.
6. Susceptible to peer-group but not adult pressure.
7. Concentration severely limited.
8. Self-effacing.
9. Distrusts, but often demands, customary schoolbook symbols of literacy.
10. Possesses invisible parents.
11. Takes little apparent pride in own work.
12. (a) Expects and accepts failure.
    (b) 'Inherits' failure from parents.
13. Needs to perceive immediate relationship between cause and effect.
14. Possesses no accomplishments.

*Like most such lists, this contains some curious juxtapositions and the few specifically grammatical features referred to appear somewhat arbitrary.

†This is curiously put but is evidently a variant of the idea of several linguists that the possession of language delays 'animal' response. Violence by an adolescent may be seen as testifying not only to the prevailing mores: but also to the absence of any perceived alternative.

15. Rarely complains.
16. Lacks conventional knowledge and experience.
17. Distrusts verbal communication.
18. Functions badly in activities of the imagination.
19. Reacts suspiciously to praise and indifferently to criticism.
20. Seldom attempts to manipulate people for advantage.
21. Lack of initiative in response.

Language habits

1. Speaks in a very limited vocabulary.
2. Reproduces sounds inaccurately.
3. Misnames objects or omits naming them.
4. Speaks haltingly without physical defect.
5. Often speaks in monotone.
6. Indiscriminate in both noisy and quiet responses.
7. Seldom or never asks questions.
8. Constantly uses present tense.
9. Seldom uses modifiers.
10. Cause and effect relationships absent in speech.
11. Rarely engages in dialogue with adults.
12. Talks almost exclusively about things.
13. Avoids situations which require words.
14. Tells transparent lies.
15. Distrusts vocal people, especially those who use 'big' words.
16. Exhibits too ready agreement.
17. Cannot easily transfer abstracted information into concrete usage.
18. Unable to vary language with situation.
19. Reluctant to move from oral to written language.

To these stereotypes another Working Party at Walsall added the following:

Speech

a. Inability to communicate at all because the whole situation is too unfamiliar or demanding (symptom found in younger children).

b. Inability to communicate in more than restricted code/ghetto language.

c. Keenness to communicate once good contact is made but restrictions caused by poverty of words and structures, with reliance on gesture. Basic concepts inadequately realized.

Listening

d. Difficulties with understanding many words, language structures, concepts.
e. Difficulties in understanding nuances of language, differences of register, etc.

Resultant reading and writing blocks

a. Problems with phonics.
b. History of early start to failure.
c. Non-literate background, hostility to books.

Resultant intellectual retardation

Problems derived from lack of experience in working things out in language. Inadequate conceptualization, etc.

Social and psychological factors

a. Cultural conflict – two societies, etc.
b. Adult–authority conflict and suspicion.
c. Problems of self-esteem, self-image, paramount need for some success.
d. Difficulties of adaptations to new situations, e.g. child's role in a class, short spans of concentration, etc.

This list of characteristics and symptoms of disadvantage may serve by virtue of its length alone – and it is not exhaustive – to give some idea of the predicament of the teacher. Certainly ten years' teaching experience in industrial areas left me quite unequipped to deal, for twenty minutes or so, with such a situation. This happened during my programme of visits to primary schools when I looked after just over half a remedial class of thirty-four seven and eight year olds while the teacher, Mrs Scholl, was taking a singing practice. The six Pakistanis were very quiet and submissive, four or five Jamaicans a bit exuberant – neither group presenting any serious problem – but the 'grey' children who made up the remainder looked like something from an illustration in an early edition of Dickens, or Kingsley. Again, most of these were manageable – just clamant and somewhat hen-witted – but a small group, including a lad who smelt strongly of cat's urine, were as beyond my control as a family of monkeys would have been. One boy seemed to like it better with most of his clothes off, while another never ceased to crawl round the room, under desks, over them. The rest didn't like him much, and at one point, when I was trying to read to them and all were relatively still – not attentive, just still – a neighbour dealt him quite without warning a fierce blow in the stomach. He cried for two minutes, I suppose, made a few retaliatory gestures before something distracted him and then, when the bell released us all only a minute later, he passed by his attacker without any apparent recollection of the injury he'd suffered. I don't think anything has brought home to me so forcefully the sense of my own alienness. I should have been gunning for my assailant for a week; for him violence was so much a part of this inexplicable cosmos that you retaliated if you remembered. Now Mrs Scholl was more capable than I of dealing with this class, but even while marvelling at her sustained pleasantness I saw enough to know the strain she was under. That very morning, she told me, one of the kids had called her an ''ffing bastard'. In this sort of situation, the observer is struck above all by the sheer physical wear and tear that is involved. Presumably this teacher was enabled to keep going by her sense of humour and her own family life after school.

I don't think that Miss Low, who came from the North and taught in the next room, had any such advantage; she probably retired each evening to a flat or bedsitter and – amazingly – emerged from it each morning. I say 'amazingly' because for me a gas fire might have presented an irresistible attraction. No, I do not think I am exaggerating or over-dramatizing; I am simply trying to imagine her predicament as I saw it, as it really was. If my tone becomes a little emotional, the reader must excuse me; it is hard to watch situations like hers for long without feeling deep anger. For she cared, and she was a good and experienced teacher.

Her class was a little smaller than average for that area – perhaps only thirty-six children – made up of third- and fourth-year (nine and ten year old) 'remedial' children, though for all Miss Low's skill and insight it was difficult to see how anything could be remedied in such a situation. I can remember her clearly – longish fair hair, fine bone structure, and eyes that showed the strain of caring impotence. This is not to imply that her back was to the wall: there was considerable order in the high-windowed, Victorian echo-chamber that was her classroom. And the kids sensed her apparently calm sympathy and respect and returned it. Almost certainly some of them loved her. The classroom had been brightened by whatever displays she had been able to help the kids devise and which she had mounted in the darkening evenings of darkened days. They drew a lot, and she was encouraging them to move from this to the verbal description of experience. She knew by training and intuition what needed to be done but, apart from a peripatetic teacher who took the Pakistanis two or three mornings a week, she was alone as she tried to help and teach the rest of the class who sat there – a daunting concatenation of inarticulate human need.

The strength of this need is suggested, in schools like Miss Low's, by the friendliness of most children who will gather round a visitor like amiable locusts. If you tell them a story they will climb over each other in an attempt to sit next to you. Physical contact assumes a particular importance when it is the only kind available. If this is pathetic, how much more so is the behaviour of those who have ceased to try to make contact. Jimmy, in Mrs Scholl's class, for example, was not normally disruptive but always took ages to decide what to get on with. When reprimanded by the teacher, however, he sat there saying nothing with a kind of explosive intensity, and banged his desk lid again and again.

More typical was Anthony, in the infants' reception class at another school nearby. Here most of the kids tried to touch me, even to say 'Hello', though after this they went silent and round-eyed, as if aghast at their own audacity. Anthony had a severe speech impediment similar to his father's. His mother and brother spoke correctly but his mother, having learnt to understand his idiolect, made no attempt to correct him. The teacher tried to help him say words correctly but she explained to me, as she tied a dozen or so pairs of shoe-laces, that there was no chance of responding adequately to his needs. Just before break I heard him recite a nursery rhyme, quite fluently and loudly. And I didn't understand enough to be able to tell what nursery rhyme it was; there seemed to be a restriction of perhaps 30 per cent in his available consonants. He came back to the classroom shortly before the end of that break, eloquently and predictably alone. He stood by the door for some long seconds, looking fixedly at me with runny nose and watery eyes upturned. And he stroked my hand several times.

Seeing him, one could only wonder at a local system that decreed that he could not see a speech therapist until he reached the age of seven. By then he would doubtless constitute a problem worthy of any therapist's mettle. No – that's, I hope, unfair: it may just be an effect of a shortage of speech therapists in that area. But it is not comfortable to know that when a child behaves like that he has needs you can't satisfy. Like the teacher in the poem, you would like to give Anthony a shilling. Because you can look into his future and you don't enjoy the godlike prescience that shows you the road he will travel to maladjustment. At the moment at least he is still touching you but by the time two years have gone by, largely occupied by reading training in which you know he will be totally lost, what efforts to establish contact will he be making?

I have written about Anthony largely because I can't forget him. That is not the only reason, however, for he exhibits in extreme form symptoms of a universal need to communicate. And, under present conditions, the teacher can recognize but often cannot meet this need.

This is why, if some aspects of a school seem repressive, we should hesitate before criticizing those who in their inability to do something positive are forced merely to preserve some comfort. Too often when we see something which we are tempted to brand as bad teaching, we are witnessing the last stages in a process of demoralization: too many compromises with harsh reality lead inexorably to a loss of sense of direction. Perhaps, given a few more years of compromise between what is desirable and what is practicable, Miss Low may appear to someone as a poor teacher. The very fact that such a thing can be envisaged underlines the seriousness of the situation.

No feature of this is more disturbing than the continuing acceptance of larger classes in primary than in secondary schools. In 1965 the Plowden Report estimated the average size of a class as 20·8 at secondary level, 28·4 at primary. Things may have improved, but only marginally, for the popular concept of the teaching profession as a two-caste system, with the primary teacher viewed as some kind of semi-skilled worker, has undergone no fundamental change. Moreover, average figures disguise frightening regional variations; in some areas the education authorities (or the ratepayers, perhaps) tolerate infant classes of forty-five while continuing to assume that the proper size of a sixth form should be ten to fifteen. In 1965 over 680,000 children (or 17 per cent of the primary population) were still being educated – if that is the right word – in primary classes of forty or more. Discrepancies of this kind defy rational explanation but must partly depend upon equating feasible numbers with the intellectual complexity of the instruction to be given. It is time we disposed of the persistent assumption that the really important things in education were like the elaborate icing – the final touches of the master – upon a cake that any honest cook would be ashamed of.

In view of the figures it cites, the comments of the Plowden Report are mild, and the diplomatic acknowledgement of the various difficulties results in proposals which lack the necessary urgency. As far back as 1931 a consultative committee 'rejected the idea that primary school classes should be larger than those for children over the age of eleven'. Thirty-six years later, the Plowden Report endorses their view yet *with some diffidence* . . .

we do not think it practicable to suggest the exact number to which primary-school classes should be reduced during the next decade and even beyond. We believe, nevertheless, that, as a general rule the maximum size of primary-school classes should be the same as that in the first two or three years of the secondary school. . . .

The Secretary of state has declared his sympathy with an ultimate objective for a class size of 'say thirty/thirty' for primary and secondary schools. We have studied the ways in which teachers and ancillary helpers are and should be used in the primary school and have come to the conclusion that a class teacher cannot satisfactorily work with more than thirty to thirty-five children.

For all teachers except the few who can work miracles, the best that can be achieved in a class of thirty-five or more is custodial. This has vital implications for language in the classroom. When we remember that the child's educability is largely dependent on his early language development, discrepancies that were not tolerable in 1931 now seem little short of criminal.

We have seen something of the diversity of the uses of language that are natural to the young child – as part of social ritual, for personal expression, to interpret experience, for explanatory communication, for accompanying action, for regulating behaviour, for play (words to mess around with reality, words as sounds to savour). These are just some of the known uses of language that have often been largely ignored in schools. For them to do better, however, some further reduction of class size seems essential.

What continued acceptance of oversize classes means for language in the classroom needs to be spelt out. Large numbers force upon the teacher an authoritarian role so that for most of the time the child becomes a receiver of only generalized, i.e. impersonal, language; the possibility of warm 'individuated' chat is reduced. This restriction on the way in which the teacher can relate to individuals within the class has two further consequences: in the first place, his potential as a listener and as a partner or participator, working alongside a child or small group of children, is drastically reduced; secondly, he is prevented from discovering enough about individuals to prescribe appropriately (reading material for example), and diversification of activity becomes progressively more difficult. All this means a drastic limitation of the range of linguistic experience the child can hope for in the classroom and this must have various effects upon his learning. Some of these are implicit in what has already been said but it is worth recalling the idea of thought as 'inner speech'. Such 'speech' must depend upon the level of language 'outside'; if the effect of large numbers is to restrict the range of language experience open to the child, and especially, the number of ways in which he can relate linguistically to an informed adult, we may expect his learning performance to suffer accordingly.

Smaller classes on their own are not enough, however. There needs to be a clearer understanding of the way in which the school as a whole constitutes a language environment. What this means, in general terms, is brought out by John Coe in a briefing paper for the Walsall Seminar in which he contrasts two such environments. In the 'old' (though not extinct) environment the children were usually:

Immobile in their desks, armed only with pens, pencils and paper, busy for so many hours filling in someone else's blanks. Do you remember? The children used to have Busy Books. It passed the time away.

The best children of course were those who were quiet. 'Wonderful class that 3A', we would say. 'They don't make a sound.' The talk, so fundamental to all language development, had to go on surreptitiously in the corridor before the lesson began, out of the side of the mouth during Morning Assembly, in the lines formed with military precision before leading in from the playground. Retribution followed discovery, 'talking' was a reason for punishment.

In the 'new' (increasingly common, but by no means universal) the activity was of a different kind:

There are children in what was once a hallowed and unused entrance hall. A group are clustered around the display unit, absorbed in making notes about a collection of African masks and carvings borrowed from the children's homes and local museums. Nearby other children are busy with books taken from bookcases surrounding a comfortable sitting area furnished with easy chairs. Here are kept the most precious and expensive books, the atlases, dictionaries and encyclopedia which cannot be duplicated in the classroom. The corridor too is being used by children.

The classrooms contain a similar range of activities with perhaps a greater emphasis on the quieter aspects of school life. We see the teacher moving among the children, working with a boy here, or a girl there, or perhaps with a group, exercising all the art of a teacher but doing so with David and Mary and not merely talking to that impersonal thing, the class.

Above all, everywhere we see and hear language in use as a real and living thing. These children, through their involvement in school life, indeed they are so involved they help to determine the course of it, are acquiring and using skills of a high order. The dominance of the textbook has lessened, the book remains but much more as one of the resources which back up the children's own exploration and discovery rooted in experience.

The language environment that a school provides is the product of several factors in particular – the teachers' attitude to the children's own lives, interests and resources; and the value teachers place upon the skills and material to be mastered, to say nothing of ways they seek to modify pupil behaviour. There are still schools in depressed areas which rely too heavily on middle-class concepts of acceptable speech and behaviour, schools where the child is so obsessed with getting the preliminaries right – 'Please, Sir/Miss/Madam ... excuse me, Sir/Miss/Madam ...' that he frequently forgets what he had been going to say. In such circumstances I doubt whether the common practice of collecting together, and thus isolating, the specially backward or deprived in 'remedial' classes can be effective. Such a practice limits the experience of children so isolated to the levels of social language that operate in a remedial class – the only factor that can raise this level being the teacher's talk.

This is not to deny a place for remedial procedures but merely to suggest that they are unlikely to succeed within a generally unsatisfactory language environment – they need as it were to be grafted to a healthy stock. Health, in this context, is not just a matter of class size, of curriculum content or of teaching method. John Coe, in the briefing paper already quoted, underlines the significant features of the 'new' environment:

Out of direct experience in life the children draw a thread of abstraction and thus symbols are given meaning. The rows of immobile children scratching away at desks have gone and in their place we have children who use both spoken and written language for expression and communication. Their words are the starting point in the building of techniques and disciplines. First the skill is used, however imperfectly, because it is part of an exciting school life, then the skill is polished and improved. How very much more appropriate this is to children who come to school without resources of their own.

Relationships too have changed in the school of today. The old authoritarianism, or at best paternalism, is giving way to a more open link with the children.... The class teacher in the primary school is fulfilling a valuable dual role. Firstly, he is coordinator of the curriculum, and through him the unity of learning, so completely natural to the child, can be achieved. Secondly, and even more importantly, through warm relationships achieved as the result of prolonged contact with the child over a period of time, he provides the security and support which everyone needs and which are needed overwhelmingly by those who come from impoverished backgrounds.

This may seem an ideal situation, but a substantial and steadily increasing number of schools offer an atmosphere which has much in common with the picture Coe presents. Such changes in the pattern of relationships lead to a marked improvement in the language environment that the school provides; as the evidence surveyed in chapter two suggests, we may expect this in turn to have an impact upon the children's learning. Coe's emphasis on language as a 'real and living thing' reminds us, moreover, that in this environment language is being made to fulfil a range of functions where it is motivated and linked to real situations, as opposed to what James Britton has called 'dummy runs'.

One cautionary note must, however, be sounded: it is possible to adopt novel methods that increase interest and improve motivation without recognizing that these are the *effects* as well as the *cause* of an improved language environment. The features of changed methods that we most often refer to are not always the most fundamental ones. This is particularly true of changes affecting the school's organization. These tend to be labelled in ways which may draw attention to relatively superficial features; there is more to the idea of the 'extended day', for example, than that it goes on longer than usual.

Rather similarly, we may find a considerable difference between a head's description of his school and what is actually going on. Of the two most effective schools seen during my tour, one was run by a head who spoke about education in conventionally 'liberal' terms, the other by one who rather prided himself on doing nothing of the kind. One could, it is true, find characteristic emphases that distinguished the two schools – the first probably encouraged expressive work more, the second placed greater emphasis on routine and systematic practice – but this is only part of the truth. Very good expressive work went on in the second school, and the 'drill', that the head-master referred to rather misleadingly from time to time, turned out to mean intensive practice designed specially for any *individual* who needed it. Equally, beneath the superficially more modern methods employed at the first school, the place of routine was clearly recognized.

This last point is worth dwelling on for a moment. Several speakers at the Walsall Seminar were critical of schools that underestimated, in their zealous application of modern educational methods, the place of routine and ritual in creating frameworks within which the often insecure deprived child finds it comfortable to work. Some of the assumptions of the Plowden Report about children's 'play' in nursery schools were based, it was argued, upon patterns of behaviour characteristic rather of the middle-class child than of all children. This is not altogether surprising, as a large proportion of nursery and play-groups – where methods have been tried out and observed – exist in precisely the areas of *least* need.*

The complex problem of the kind of frameworks a child needs is not clarified by the adoption of simplistic 'pro-routine' positions. Routine in itself is not something to oppose or to favour; it can be invested with quite different values and assumptions about children. Routines can be enforced *upon* children, designed *for* them or evolved *with* them. In some primary schools classroom routines are largely built up according to the activities and materials the children are engaged with – the use of paint, of craft materials, of books *in a communal setting*, each impose certain disciplined procedures. At a more basic level, the experience of primary teachers in some parts of London suggests that after the summer holidays it takes three to four weeks for children to re-learn how to come into the classroom and move about the school in an acceptable way. Here the routines established are to calm them down – largely by talk – and to socialize them; at first they are established to give security but later they may be used as bases from which to move towards greater freedom. In this context, one needs to emphasize the importance of the teacher's own reliability and consistency –

*For example, for the children of university staff – which is not to suggest that some of these may not be quite significantly deprived.

essential parts of any school routine. The example of the two schools I have mentioned may serve as a useful reminder that there are more ways to Jerusalem or Utopia than oversimplifications of educational theory might suggest. Their differences in fact matter less than what unites them – an emphasis on good relationships, and a belief in the fundamental importance of language development.

Secondary

The nice little curiosities and willingnesses of a child were in a jumbled and thwarted condition, ... and Mr Polly had lost much of his natural confidence, so far as figures and sciences and languages and the possibilities of learning things were concerned. He thought of the present world no longer as a wonderland of experiences, but as geography and history, as the repeating of names that were hard to pronounce, and lists of products and populations and heights and lengths, and as lists of dates – oh! and boredom indescribable (H. G. Wells, 1910).

Though this was written sixty years ago, the account of Mr Polly's educational progress is frequently echoed by primary-school teachers as they shake their heads over the change in Johnny or Willy, now that he has gone to the secondary school. And often their account not merely echoes but recalls *in detail* Wells's comments above. There may be some truth in the secondary teacher's remark that some primary teachers ascribe to the secondary school changes that are the effect of maturational processes over which the school has little or no control, but this is not the whole of the story. It is suggestive that in some areas when the young adults talk of going back to their old school, or when they *do* go back, it is to their primary not their secondary school.

The procedures of the secondary school often seem calculated to reinforce intellectual difficulties and emotional blockages that are first encountered at primary level. In a working paper for the Walsall Seminar, Professor Marjorie Smiley of Hunter College, New York, argued that at the root of these problems lay a breakdown in communication. The effect of this was to convince the child that *'what the teacher wants, what the school wants, is beyond understanding'*. Behind the statistics reporting slum children's low scores on reading and language tests, she thought, lay a series of experiences like that of a class of eight year olds as described by Gloria Channon:

Picture a lesson in rhyming words, a very useful lesson which occurs frequently in the early grades. I write the word on the board. I ask a child to say it. 'Ole,' he says. 'That's right, old. Now give me some words that rhyme with it.' 'Tole.' I know my children don't mean *toll*, so I say, 'Good,' and I write *told* on the board. 'Fole?' I record *fold*. '*Bole?*' 'Use it in a sentence.' If he should say 'The soldier is bole,' I will write it. If he should say 'Bole of cereal,' I will reject it. 'Cole' is listed: *cold*. 'Pole' is refused. 'Sole' (*sold*) is a good word. 'Role?' Never. I am beginning to be just a little impatient. Why are they so irritatingly erratic in their responses? The child, sensing my tension, is getting worried. Why do I respond so erratically to his words? His faith in himself is shaken. Perhaps I am not after what he thought I wanted, rhymes for *ole*. Now he will often give up, and I will be unable to elicit another word from him. I assume he has run through his meagre vocabulary and feels frustration and despair. Another child might notice my unhappiness at the failure of the lesson. Eager to please me, he wracks his brain for some answers that will restore my good humour. Maybe I want O words? 'Over, open,' he offers.

I do not thank him for his kind intentions. I almost sneer – 'OLD, OLD,' I repeat. He picks out another sound, perhaps even the D which I have drummed out so emphatically this time. 'Did, doll, load.' No use (Channon, 1968, p. 7).

While the breakdown of communication often begins in the primary school, the situation of the child as he attempts to adjust to the new demands of the secondary school is calculated to exacerbate his difficulties. In many instances the social situation and the learning procedures in the secondary school are different enough to arouse acute anxieties in thoroughly normal children. Often, too, the school is at loggerheads with the surrounding community, and the mutual hostility often latent at primary level becomes fairly explicit. In its mildest form, this means that pupils will tend to think of the world of school as unreal but often teachers and pupils see each other's background and values as constituting what Dan Fader has called an 'adversary culture'.

Some of our older schools are found in areas where this gulf has been so long accepted that the people and many of the teachers can hardly envisage any other kind of relationship between school and community. It was in such an area that I came upon a secondary school for girls. Even the architecture seemed to emphasize the school's defensive stance – it would have come as no surprise to learn that a portcullis or even a moat had only recently been dispensed with: in short, a perfect companion piece for the school which Edward Blishen evoked so vividly in *Roaring Boys* (1966). I found the headmistress trying to tidy up some of the previous week's troubles.

On Friday there had been a whole series of thefts, some of them senseless. It was not long since four girls had attacked the teacher of a fourth-year class and had gone on causing trouble until dispersed to other schools; now another teacher of the same class had had her hair pulled by another four whose sole intention was clearly to reduce her to tears and humiliation. Such things, the headmistress recalled, had been quite common eighteen months earlier so that she had learnt to expect and to deal with injured teachers as well as the common run of hurt children. More usually now the violence was below the surface and the major weapon was well-drilled dumb insolence. A few weeks earlier, for example, a teacher who had taken a group of girls to play rounders stood helpless as they silently walked away and finally disappeared.

Disappearing – or not appearing – was part of the girls' normal routine. Absenteeism was a hallowed local tradition, said the headmistress with a wry smile. In the school as a whole the rate of absenteeism was 40 per cent, but probably 50 per cent in the lower of the two streams in each year. Sometimes absences followed a regular pattern – in one class, for instance, she expected at least nine girls out of twenty to be absent every Monday afternoon. In a situation where it was extremely difficult to get even a part-time school secretary, they could have employed a full-time social worker. A few facts drove her point home: in the first year, at least 25 per cent of the lower group had criminal fathers; in the corresponding second-year group alone, seven out of twenty kids came from broken West Indian homes; of the third-year group five girls had been sent to special schools, four had been suspended. Many of the kids were seriously hurt or disturbed – perhaps a quarter, she thought. In the lower third-year class only four girls could read enough to do an assignment or group work. She would have liked to do a crash course on reading throughout the school but the senior English mistress was not interested in the lower groups.

Like about a quarter of the staff, that teacher had been there for too long and, having established a routine that rendered her own life tolerable, was anxious to preserve the *status quo*. Merely to endure in that environment for fifteen years, and several had endured longer than that, must take its toll of emotional response. I wondered if, thirty years before, any of them had been like Miss Low.* It seemed possible. Even the tall one, with the metallic voice and iron-grey hair who had been implacably directing children into the hall when I arrived, had looked through me and away again, even she. . . . What can it be like to love one's subject and teach in such a school?

'It's no place for starry-eyed new teachers. . . .' There was perhaps a hint of bitterness in the head's voice. 'It's not cynical' – she said unnecessarily – 'but I think the school should be closed. Formal discipline is not feasible . . . you have to play it by ear – there are no rules. You've got to be . . . relaxed.' She shrugged sadly as if realizing the impossibility of that. 'It's no place for an insecure teacher!'

It is quite common to hear the transition from primary to secondary school – from a system with a stable class teacher to one with subject specialists, to whom pupils go for brief periods of instruction unrelated to what has gone before – described as 'traumatic'. It must be so when a child comes to such a school as this. The environment has determined that she arrives with a language deficit, ill-equipped to meet the school's demands; the problem of coping with subject specialists is exacerbated by frequent staff changes; and, finally, there is the incompatibility of the culture represented by the school with that of the surrounding area.

These conditions may usefully remind us that unfeasible teaching situations are not confined to primary schools. Moreover, though this school is hardly typical even of schools in very deprived areas, the kind of difficulties it faced have much in common with those suggested by the official inquiries into the

* See p. 80.

teaching of our less able children that made up the Newsom Report. Despite an accelerated building programme, it remains doubtful how far the problems that Newsom drew attention to – in particular, the high turnover of staff in deprived areas and the tendency to allocate weak or inexperienced teachers to diffi-cult classes – have been solved. High staff turnover is often deplored because it means that the children who most need it are denied a stable relationship with an adult. It is in itself also a *language* problem, however. For the more fortunate, stable teachers provided language models; the unfortunate child there-fore lacks more than a significant relationship with an adult – he lacks the opportunity to relate to an adult *speaker*.

In recent years we have come to recognize that even under more normal circumstances, the child may find the change from primary to secondary school difficult. Two kinds of solution have been proposed. The first type, following the lead given in the Plowden Report, seeks to relate the ages of transition from one level to another to observable developmental stages. Schools for the eight-plus to twelve-plus age range suggested by Plow-den are still relatively rare, however, and a second type of solu-tion to the problem of transition has found considerable support; this avoids radical change in the traditional pattern of schooling, relying instead upon the modifications of both cur-riculum and teaching method. Thus many schools now attempt to smooth the transition by making the first two years of secon-dary schooling a logical development, in content and method, of work at primary level. This has involved not only a much-needed rethinking of curricula, but also an attention to teaching method and to pastoral care. Thus, for example, there is a ten-dency to retain something of the class-teacher system or at any rate to decrease the constant shunting of children from one group to another.

Despite the thought that has gone into these developments, however, the problems of primary–secondary transition have been only partially understood. Here a contributing factor has been the preoccupation with the comprehensive debate: the main concern has been for children moving from small primary to vast secondary schools, and attention has been concentrated upon the disorientation that such a change may produce. Discussion has been preoccupied with the methods – feasible or otherwise – *of settling the child in*. In this connection even those who speak from experience (as opposed to speculation) have been misled by the facility with which children adopt 'survival strategies'. It is true that children do not like to be socially uncomfortable, but they find few things more uncomfortable than having their discomfort recognized. This means that they concentrate hard on learning to fit in, in order to avoid notice. All this bears upon something called social behaviour, however, which is too often seen as distinct from what goes on in the classroom. The whole argument of chapter two throws doubt upon such a dichotomy. *The change to a new social and a new learning situation at secondary level has effects upon language – and hence upon learning – whose implications have frequently been overlooked.*

The pupil commencing his secondary-school career has lost the social security of his old primary classroom, where he worked among friends he had known for years under a teacher whose expectations he had learnt to understand in a variety of situations, ranging from English to woodwork, from elementary science to football. His problem now is not merely that of adjusting to the fact that he will be taught, in different ways, by several teachers but of acclimatizing himself to a series of new social learning situations, each of which may expose his uncertainties and strain his limited language resources. Douglas Barnes's 'Language in the secondary classroom', already referred to in chapter two, underlines the inadequacy of the concessions made to pupils who have only *begun* to adjust to a new school world. He suggests also a continuing predominance of factual learning in the early years of secondary school that is likely to contrast with the pupil's previous experience. If factual learning of this type is alien to him, however, the general attitude of teachers towards his own experience will be much more so. This attitude is shown most clearly in the kinds of question which teachers ask and which are highly effective means of modifying the pupils' behaviour:

Those children who come up from primary schools ready to explore personal experience aloud and to offer anecdotal contributions to discussion cease to do so within a few weeks of arrival. Clearly they learn in certain lessons that anecdotes are held by the teacher to be irrelevant ... because the teacher never asks questions that can be answered by anecdotes, anecdotes cease to be a part of their thinking about the subject, and become 'unthinkable' as contributions to class discussion (Barnes, Britton, Rosen and the LATE, 1971, pp. 25–6).

It is not merely that the kinds of questions asked make anecdotal responses inadmissible, however, as Barnes points out, they frequently presuppose a single correct answer, a tendency itself related closely to the predominance of factual learning. The inanities to which this kind of questioning may lead were deliciously recalled in a talk by Peter Ustinov. Recounting his schooldays, he told of the general knowledge tests he regularly had to endure; on one occasion, asked to name a Russian composer, he wrote 'Rimsky Korsakov', and was perplexed to be informed that this was wrong, the correct answer being, *of course*, 'Tchaikovsky'! General knowledge tests have become less common in school, perhaps, but the persistence of 'closed' questions suggests that the teacher's testing function remains. When Barnes's team of observers followed a first-year class, in their first term of secondary education, through a whole day's lessons, they found not one example of an 'open' question (one to which several answers would be acceptable) which did not require pupils to 'think aloud', to 'construct, or reconstruct from memory, a logically organized sequence'. In other words, even where the content of an acceptable answer is not prescribed, the style will be, for a premium is commonly placed upon certain *reasoned* ways of responding. The following incident, which occurred early in my wife's teaching career, suggests that what happens when a teacher asks a 'closed' question is more complicated than is often assumed.

The headmaster's custom was to 'keep tabs' on new teachers by popping into their classes, without warning, and thrusting in his own, often somewhat disconcerting, oar. On this occasion he listened for a few moments to a discussion of the Parable of the Sower with a mixed fourth-year class of signally unacademic disposition – a class who, perhaps because of their profound uninterest, constituted the seventh stream. The class seemed to the head slow to realize what intense heat meant. His intervention – based, one can only assume, on some idea of contrasts –

was surprising, however.

Why – he thundered, in his rich Black-Country accent – why do you think the Eskimo man and wife share the same sleeping bag?

There was a silence. If the class were taken aback by the interruption, they were stunned as the implications of the question began to dawn upon them. The silence lengthened.

Impatiently – trying to simplify it for minds that were evidently simple – the head repeated his question.

Why, in Greenland, among the Eskimos, do the man and his wife get into the same sleeping bag?

With difficulty the bonds of conventional discipline held; my wife noted several members of the class in evident discomfort, but the silence was maintained. Indeed, the attention of the class was riveted upon the questioner in a way that a novice might mistakenly have found flattering, evidence of the interest he had skilfully aroused. In the end he capitulated. Shaking his head at their massive stupidity, he roared the answer he had sought:

Why, to keep warm of course!

The anecdote is interesting not merely as an example of the superhuman restraint exercised by thirty-eight normally irreverent adolescents, nor indeed as a classic example of a *closed* question, expecting a single predetermined answer: more than this, it illustrates the complexity of what goes on in the classroom. Thus a simple question leads not to a simple answer of the kind that must have occurred naturally and immediately (though perhaps in cruder form) to 90 per cent of this class, viz, 'to copulate in comfort', but to the formulation of a quite different question – 'What's he up to: what's his game now?' The original question has to be reinterpreted in terms of previous experience of (a) the questioner himself, (b) the situation, (c) any non-verbal clues the speaker may give.

My example of a closed question may appear untypical or unlikely, however, so let us look at an illustration from a lesson in religious education that Barnes describes:

The teacher was asking for the recall of information about life in New Testament Palestine.

T   How did they get water from the well? ... do you remember?
    ... Yes?
P.1 They ... ran the bucket down ... er ... and it was fastened on to
    this bit of string and it ... [here the words become inaudible for
    a phrase or two] ... other end to the water.
T   You might do it that way ... where did they put the water ...
    John?
P.2. In a big ... er ... pitcher.
T   Good ... in a pitcher ... which they carried on their ...?
P   Heads.

The question 'How did they get the water from the well?' has
signalled to Pupil 1 that this is a relatively open question to which an
improvised sequence would be appropriate. His reply, the quality of
which is here irrelevant, is met by 'You might do it that way'
spoken with an intonation expressing doubt. That is, Pupil 1's
answer is rejected, though in a polite form of words. Pupil 2 suggests
an answer *of a different kind*; he intuits – or remembers – that his
teacher does not want improvised reasoning but the name of an object. His reply 'In a big ... er ... pitcher' is accepted and carried
further with a promptness which signals to both pupils that this is
what was required in the first place. It might be surmised that these
pupils are not only learning about Palestine but also about the kinds
of reciprocal behaviour appropriate to a teacher–pupil relationship,
that is, learning when not to think. (It should be remembered that
they are in their sixth week in a new school.)

This is an example of the kind of question which the investigators
have come to call a 'pseudo-question', in that while it has the form
of an open question the teacher's treatment of replies shows that he is
willing to accept only one answer (Barnes, Britton, Rosen and the
LATE, 1971, pp. 33–4).

Barnes's illustrations from a religious education lesson, short
though it is, recalls vividly an experience of my own. On this
occasion I was sitting with a first-year class through their morning's lessons. A lesson in oral Franch which was lively and
apparently enjoyable was followed by Religious Education. The
atmosphere in the RE lesson was noticeably different. The
teacher, who gave an impression of cold vigilance, talked in a
business-like way about the settlement of Canaan by the Israel-
ites, showing the names of the tribes, from Asher to Zebulon,
on a map he had drawn on the blackboard. My growing unease
during this ten- to fifteen-minute introduction was caused not

merely by the consciousness that all this was remarkably remote in time and space from the interests of the children; what was more disturbing was the frequency with which alien adult concepts – 'boundaries' for example – occurred in the course of what was intended to be an explanation addressed to a class whose average 'reading-age' was about *seven years eight months*. For the last ten to fifteen minutes of the lesson they had to copy the map on the board. As I looked around me at the blank faces poring submissively over meaningless and wildly inaccurate maps, the conviction grew that this was an exercise whose sole value – like the teacher's talk – was as part of a conditioning process designed to render pupils quiescent.

This process begins, of course, as soon as pupils discover that some hitherto quite normal language strategies are no longer open to them in the secondary school. Barnes's reference to the way anecdotes become 'unthinkable' is a case in point and the tendency to increasingly passive pupil behaviour is clearly accelerated by the kinds of question the teacher asks. If the teacher's questions are one indication of the speech climate in a classroom, however, so too are the pupils' questions. In his survey Barnes was struck both by their rarity and by their limited scope: what questions were forthcoming tended to be requests for clarification about the task in hand, and symptomatic of a desire for reassurance rather than information. Most teachers will recognize this type: 'Does it have to be in best books? How long should it be? Will a poem do? Can I write in biro?'

In passing, it is worth emphasizing that a preponderance of such questions, so far from being a symptom of a linguistic restriction peculiar to 'disadvantaged' children *is most commonly found in the junior forms of our most academic schools*. These will often place a premium on conformist behaviour, will rely upon predominantly authoritarian modes of instruction and will be attended by children who are often *over-motivated* and hence prone to every kind of anxiety. Thus, in an apparently privileged setting, we find the conjunction of three factors that can impose serious restrictions upon learning – as a direct result of the speech climate that prevails. The pupils' evident control of the resources of an elaborated code should not blind us to the fact that the *purposes* for which that code is used may themselves be so restricted as to preclude self-discovery, initiative and new ways of thinking:

It is not enough for pupils to imitate the forms of teachers' language, as if they were models to be copied; it is only when they 'try it out' in reciprocal exchanges so that they modify the way they use language to organize reality that they are able to find new functions for language in thinking and feeling (Barnes, Britton, Rosen and the LATE, 1971, p. 61).

Barnes was criticizing the low level of pupil participation in the lessons he observed, which 'if at all typical of secondary lessons is a matter of some educational urgency'. The best comment I know upon language deprivation in our privileged schools comes from an unlikely source. In *Letter to a Teacher* some Italian peasant boys, failures in the eyes of their own system, emphasize the importance of language and also the importance of being in touch with reality in a way that is impossible for Pierino, the rich boy:

True culture, which no man has as yet possessed, would be made up of two elements: belonging to the masses and mastery of the language.
A school that is as selective as the kind we have described destroys culture. It deprives the poor of the means of expressing themselves. It deprives the rich of the knowledge of things as they are.
Unlucky Gianni, who can't express himself. Lucky Gianni, because he belongs to the whole world: brother to the whole of Africa, Asia and Latin America. Expert in the needs of most of humanity.
Lucky Pierino, because he can speak. Unlucky, because he speaks too much. He, who has nothing important to say. He, who repeats only things read in books written by others just like him (School of Barbiana, 1970, p. 89).

A classroom environment where the technical level of language competence appears high may yet be artificial enough to inhibit real learning. Queries, for example, about the length or the presentation of homework could as easily be labelled '*pseudo*-questions' as those where the teacher is expecting a single, 'right' answer. By contrast, I recall the question of a seven year old as I picked up my wife after school: approaching the car on my wife's side, she nodded rather unsubtly in my direction: 'Am that yer Dad, Miss?' she inquired with interest. *That* was a real question – the sort she would later learn not to ask teachers.

Barnes suggested that questions about procedure and requests for clarification indicated a need for reassurance. We may take this further by recalling Carl Rogers's assertion that a student needs to be psychologically 'safe' before he is 'free' to think creatively (see chapter two, p. 49). Real questions – involving a need-to-know – are by their very nature admissions about oneself, and a major concern of this chapter is with that unsensational but serious level of linguistic deprivation common to all educational environments where such admissions either cannot be attended to, or are made progressively less feasible for the pupils. The central issue is splendidly put by another American psychologist interested in classroom practices:

One has only to spend some time as a professional outsider in an elementary school to know that children will share their answers with almost anyone who asks the right questions; but they will only share their questions with their own teachers – and then only if they love them. After all, there is little risk in giving an answer; it is either right or wrong and that is usually the end of it. But to share a question is often to invite inspection of one's tenderer parts. Like other loving acts this is not something we do with strangers (Jones, 1968, p. 47).

This is not sentimentality but a pedagogic insight of profound importance. Jones had been considering the 'emotionally facilitating characteristics' which distinguished one group of lessons with ten to eleven year olds (based on a film about Eskimos) which had led to a spate of 'significant, credible and relevant questions', from another series by an equally competent teacher, using the same film, in which the children evinced only 'superficial involvement and boredom, the lesson ending in question-less silence'.

The successful teacher had been forced to set up a special procedure – 'a question-box period' – in order to *preserve* the questions, and this usefully suggests the desirability of such procedures as part of normal practice. Other critics of the American classroom emphasize the need for such strategies:

What all of us have learned (and how difficult it is to un-learn it!) is that it is not important that our utterances satisfy the demands of the question (or of reality), but that they satisfy the demands of the classroom environment. Teacher asks. Student answers. Have you ever heard of a student who replied to a question, 'Does *anyone* know the answer to that question?' or 'I don't understand what I would have to do in order to find an answer,' or 'I have been asked that question before, and, frankly, I've never understood what it meant'? Such behaviour would invariably result in some form of penalty and is, of course, scrupulously avoided, except by 'wise guys'. Thus, students learn not to value it. They get the message. And yet few teachers consciously articulate such a message. It is not part of the 'content' of their instruction. No teacher ever said: 'Don't value uncertainty and tentativeness. Don't question questions. Above all, don't think.' The message is communicated quietly, insidiously, relentlessly, and effectively through the structure of the classroom: through the role of the teacher, the role of the student, the rules of their verbal game, the rights that are assigned, the arrangements made for communication, the 'doings' that are praised or censured. In other words, the medium is the message (Postman and Weingartner, 1969, p. 33).

The authors go on to propose a new mode of study the central tenet of which is the proposition:

Once you have learned how to ask questions – relevant and appropriate and substantial questions – you have learned how to learn and no one can keep you from learning whatever you want or need to know.

This is not a new idea; it is many years since A. N. Whitehead first criticized the university student's 'aimless accumulation of knowledge, inert and unutilized'. It remains a live issue, however, and will do so as long as teachers are obsessed with the need to teach, and yet unaware of the kinds of learning that are impeded by their own unconscious language strategies.

These indeed are sometimes explicitly stated in the 'practical advice' given to students learning to teach. I remember a headmaster who began his (1968) introductory talk to a group of graduates at the beginning of teaching practice with the words: 'The important thing is to be aloof.' Later on the deputy, who looked after the female graduates in the group, underlined the point by warning them not to *smile at the boys* in class.

I can only assume that both would have thoroughly approved of a geography lesson I saw, in a poor urban area, taken with a third-year class, some, but not all, of whom might one day be entered for the CSE exam.

The lesson subject was *ocean currents round Japan*. The introduction of the lesson occupied perhaps three minutes and was delivered in school-masterful manner, tinged with sardonic humour:

'I only show this to favoured people; I don't know why I'm showing it to you.'

For perhaps the next twenty minutes the class with the help of atlases engaged themselves in putting 'labels' on duplicated blank maps, while the teacher wandered round the class making comments not unkindly but couched in an archetypal pedagogic style:

'It could be said to be inaccurate' or 'Where have you got that strange word from?'

In response to some questions early in his wanderings he was moved to address his answer to the whole class:

'The whole point (of labelling the ocean currents) is that when the time comes, as come it will, you shall be able to do the whole thing *from memory*.'

What follows from aloofness, and the correspondingly passive behaviour of pupils, is not 'concentration' as some would have us believe (to be quiet = to be getting on with it) but an increase in irrelevant learning. For the child, aloofness means that it is hard to tune in, impossible to ask certain kinds of questions; he is therefore forced to adopt various survival strategies which have more to do with 'reading the situation' than with intellectual endeavour. For the teacher, an aloof stance involves inevitably aloofness of language. This assumes a psychological distance between teacher and taught, eliminating the whole range of activities in which he might work with or alongside children and, consequently, the whole range of related language uses.

In this context, however, we need to beware of over-simplification. It is true that habitual remoteness usually goes with an over-emphasis on both routine and teaching material. But this does not mean that we are to approve only teachers who are, for example, exuberant or extrovert. Children pick up different signals from different types of teacher and are sensitive to more than one kind of indication of respect, sympathy or concern. Not only does one meet a wide variety of demeanour amongst *effective* teachers, but also in a particular teacher. There are probably occasions when aloofness is right – certainly there are times when the teacher has to guard himself as a person. Teachers need to distance children differently from moment to moment, and the language will match the varying situation – again extending the child's experience and, as he learns to respond appropriately, his active speech repertoire. What was really wrong with the headmaster's advice to those graduates was not that he was pro-aloofness (where we are anti-) but that he didn't understand the need for flexibility.

At the start of their teaching practice students quite often receive from senior staff advice which conflicts with their training or their intuition. Some of the most misleading 'practical tips' are given not so much by teachers embittered by work in specially difficult conditions as by those whose own secure systems appear challenged by modern developments. In this situation, a teacher lacking confidence and uncertain what his role should be may give 'reactionary' advice in order to defend himself. One of the most influential books on English teaching, Frank Whitehead's *The Disappearing Dais* (1966), elaborates the way the teacher's role changes once he is prepared to descend from his platform of authority. This development is now well established though by no means universally accepted in the field of English, but in some other subjects the process of change has only begun. It is natural for such changes to produce anxiety. The old dais had its own clear-cut style; it is hard to speak intimately from a platform. The teacher who has 'descended' now finds that confusion about his role leads to confusion about his language.

In his attempt to adjust to the changes that are 'in the air' perhaps the biggest single disadvantage the secondary teacher has to face is the series of assumptions about the classroom environment that are the product of his own experience as both learner and teacher. The architecture and even the furniture of the classroom to which he has grown accustomed have bred in him the notion that his responsibility is towards a group or class – a number of individuals that may be considered as a unit.* Hence the extreme pains taken even in comprehensive schools to arrange homogeneous – i.e. 'teachable' – groups. Whatever the advantages of such grouping – and there are some – the insidious results upon the teacher's behaviour and expectations are plain. It becomes more and more difficult to see the thirty-six *individuals* in front of him. When we add to this his lack of confidence in using techniques that are designed for teaching *individuals* we produce a vicious circle. He can't see the individual, so blinkered is he by his own conditioning; the same conditioning makes him feel unable to teach the individual even if he can locate him.

A further factor reinforces the tendency to look at groups rather than individuals. I referred in chapter one to the tendency for children who at primary school are seen as victims to be regarded as culprits by the time they reach secondary school. Now if it is unhappy to contemplate thirty-six victims, it is unnerving to face thirty-six culprits. It is not so much the physical threat that matters, serious problem though this is in certain areas, but the threat to the teacher's self-esteem which inevitably limits his capacity to discriminate between individuals. A remarkable play by Giles Cooper (orginally broadcast on the Third Programme) called *Unman, Wittering and Zigo,* traces the events in a classroom as a new teacher gradually discovers what happened to his predecessor – the class in fact murdered him. Here again, what is horrible is not the physical threat but the inexorable way in which the class undermines the teacher's morale. In any circumstance where the teacher is confronted, as many are, by verbally threatening behaviour, survival depends upon a security largely based on knowing quite clearly who he is, and why he is there. To succeed, rather than merely survive, the teacher's inner security must be sufficient for him to retain his capacity to discriminate between the various needs of those in front of him.

The teacher's difficulties are increased by the fact that, though we may spare the rod or use modern teaching materials, basic assumptions about the teacher's functions have undergone little

*'The notion that there is a "front of the class" and the authoritarian mode of delivering knowledge received from above to students who are below both go together' (Kohl, 1969).

radical change. Advice to young teachers – such as that about aloofness – testifies to this, as Herbert Kohl discovered when he began his teaching career.

The entire staff of the school was obsessed by 'control', and beneath the rhetoric of faculty meetings was the clear implication that students were a reckless, unpredictable, immoral and dangerous enemy (Kohl, 1969, p. 13).*

Rather similarly, I have known student teachers summoned to a staff meeting only to leave it an hour or two later with no very clear idea of what it had all been about. They all had the impression that the management was dissatisfied with them but it took another hour's discussion for them to conclude that the source of the dissatisfaction lay in the conviction that noise in a classroom = loss of control.

The relevance of this to language development (and hence to learning) is not simply that if noise spells danger, talk will be avoided. The restriction upon language derives also from the setting up of a context for social learning which apparently offers both teacher and taught only two options – to control, or to be controlled. Paradoxically, an obsession with control tends to generate precisely those problems that are most feared. Finally, it must be emphasized that, though 'control' carries an implication of strong-arm tactics, the strategies most commonly employed are linguistic – domination by mystification, by aloofness, by sarcasm.

Such then are a few of the factors that obstruct the teacher's vision of the individual and force him to look at a group of bodies. The results are seen in stereotyping. We all know the influence of the mass media in this connection, insidiously leading us to feel for instance that long hair and moral dependability are incompatible. The classroom orientation of schools is such as to reinforce this tendency to erect quite unreal norms and regard those who depart from them not as original individualists but as deviants. This has led to widespread schoolmaster's neurosis

*Even closed questions may themselves have a controlling function. Ustinov's sense of grievance at gaining no marks for answering 'Rimsky-Korsakov' instead of 'Tchaikovsky' was deepened when he discovered himself an object of some suspicion thereafter. He was marked out as being 'clever' in a way that might be *subversive*.

which appears to the outsider in the form of lunatic obsessions with trivia – with the kind of ties boys wear, or how they tie them, with pointed shoes, leather belts and, of course, hairstyles.

If both teacher and taught are used to either controlling or being controlled, it follows that the student or the raw, new teacher who is genuinely interested in the pupils' responses is liable to have this openness misinterpreted by everybody as weakness or permissiveness. Kohl's own testimony here is particularly valuable, not merely because he was working in a setting where authoritarian assumptions were normal but also because he was an inexperienced teacher in a very deprived area. Progress was hard to achieve but began as a result of apparently simple techniques designed to bring the teacher into new meaningful contact with individuals:

– talk to students outside class.
– watch them play and watch them live with other young people.
– play with them – joking games and serious games.
– talk to them about yourself, what you care about.
– listen.

As a result, Kohl suggests, 'the kids may surprise you and reveal rather than conceal as is usual in the classroom, their feelings, playfulness and intelligence' (1969, p. 22). When such openness is a characteristic of the classroom, the results are far-reaching. Kohl quotes the testimony of another experienced teacher on this point:

once teachers free themselves of the feeling that they 'are not teaching the kids anything', and learn to perceive as real learning the activities and questions and conversations which develop spontaneously in their classroom, they become much more confident and relaxed and many of the former problems of control simply disappear (Kohl, 1969, p. 101).

It is above all a preoccupation with teaching, conceived in narrowly conventional terms which has led to the extensive miseducation of those pupils who form the bulk of the early school leavers, and of many now trying to repair the damage in colleges of further education. From teachers whose preoccupation with control has led them to see threats where few exist – to perceive insolence in dumbness, an insult in a hesitation – such pupils have indeed *learned*. Where each side distrusts the other's verbal utterances meaningful educational communication has verbal cues – to attend to what he does, not what he says.

This is also a perfect situation for convincing the less able pupil that he's not much good. It is a curious fact that pupils can reject both a teacher and his subject, and yet accept his explicit and implied judgement upon them. It may be that this cuts too deeply for them to be rational about it. The Italian peasant boys, who wrote *Letter to a Teacher* put it simply and clearly:

For her, one boy – out of thirty-two – is just a fraction. But for the boy a teacher is much more. He had only *one* teacher, and she threw him out (School of Barbiana, 1970, p. 40).

An American boy, waiting for his sixteenth birthday so that he could leave school, was more analytical about it (reinforcing what was said about teacher expectation in chapter two):

Take my dean telling me that I'm not going to make it ... I couldn't make it ... there's no use my coming to school anyway. That's doubting me. That's showing me doubt in myself. ... That's not encouraging me to go anywhere. ... He's putting me down. So instead of picking me up he's pushing me down. Actually that's what he's doing. And that's what makes some dropouts become dropouts all their own life. You know? (Fuchs, 1966, p. 150).*

This youth's English counterparts are commonly found in what is called a fourth-year leavers' set† This depressing institution, its members bound together only by their uniform desire to leave school as soon as possible, inevitably contains individuals of widely differing ability and maturity. Quite possibly a few are there because they 'haven't got it' but the majority are pupils whose social and linguistic experience at home and in primary school has prevented them in various ways from making sense of the learning environment traditionally provided by the secondary school.

* Quoted by Professor Marjorie Smiley in her Working Paper for the Walsall Seminar.

† When we have fifth-year leavers' sets the problems may well be even more obvious.

It is surprising how few of these sets are really troublesome. The truth is, I fancy, that they no longer *care* enough to rebel. For years the victims of an unsensational but relentless deprivation, they now demonstrate an apathy that is almost mystical. After all, it won't be long now . . .; how right the headmaster who called such sets 'waiting rooms for industry'. Like a boxer who, reluctant to fight some puny opponent, dodges or rides his punches, they watch for an opportunity to slip out of the ring.

I have watched various groups of student teachers – young, sympathetic and lively – vainly wrestling to provoke a response from classes like these. The students work with carefully prepared material, based on topics 'the kids must be interested in'. The pupils watch sympathetically, recognizing genuine effort and intention, but their responses come in half-sentences. Of course the students often pitch the material at the wrong level – but it would make little difference if they got it right every time. They want to 'make contact' with the class, but the class is wiser – they know that that is not what the classroom is for. Once out of the classroom in which and to which they have been conditioned, however, their behaviour and responsiveness often change dramatically, allowing the teacher an altogether more optimistic view of their potential. I remember the difference between a leavers' set which I took in 'Room 4' and the same set taken at a local community centre. At the time it was astonishing, but it seems less so in the light of work like that of Luria and Lawton upon the effect of social environments upon language and learning.

If fourth-year leavers demonstrate the effects of in-school deprivation, however, so do many students in colleges of further education. Some of these, having 'failed' in their secondary education. Some of these, having 'failed' in their secondary fresh attempt to learn; others, among the most disadvantaged students one can find, lack any such hopeful motivation but are forced to attend classes by contract with their employers. It was a class of such compulsory 'day-release' students that David Longley described to participants at the Walsall Seminar. He had asked them to imagine a situation in which an alien 'people' in 'UFOs' took over the earth and decided that it needed cleaning up. Earth-dwellers were therefore called upon to justify their claim to continued existence. Longley noted that in discussion – when exposed before their peers and bound to keep up a 'front' – the students responded with some optimism. By contrast, when they came to *write* about it, they did so with very unoptimistic frankness:

John Richardson

If these UFO attacked and they said 'we going to killed'. Then they want an answer to why I should be kept alive and the others die. Because there nothing I can do that other people can't do, some may not just as good but some are better, because some have got GCEs.

Geoffrey Birkett

I think that the idea that the foreigners have got is a good one, they say that there is a lot of hardship on this world and that they will eliminate all the useless people on the world, if they were going to kill me I would not mind because I am fed up with living in this stupid world where you have to work for nothing, and everyone treads on you and kicks you up the arse and trys to push you about and I just don't care.

David Andrew

I don't think that I should stay alive because I am not brainy and if someone is brainier than me and can do the world some good he should stay alive but I don't think that any man or beast or creature from outer space should be allowed to kill.

These may appear relatively unremarkable expressions of failure-feelings and therein lies the danger. Our new awareness of the 'dropout problem' may produce its own stereotype. Labels are no guarantee of understanding and there is a possibility that in naming this problem we lose sight of its complexity. There are many kinds of failure, some of which – like that of the non-academic child in a conventional school – are well documented. Others may easily be ignored, however. For instance, a youth may be a failure in the eyes of his peers; the goals set by adolescent culture are not always congenial to its members. The less confident an adolescent is, the more intolerable may seem the patterns that his culture *appears* to impose on him. I say 'appears' for his vision is clouded by his very lack of confidence. Some of the most unhappy children in our schools are I suspect sensitive, immature children who feel forced to conform to an image of toughness. Many of the institutional procedures of the school reinforce them in their assumption that if they're not all alike, they ought to be. Certainly they may not accept the school's ideals or norms, but even in reacting against them their underlying assumptions about *conformity* are not shaken.

The teacher who relies on stereotypes in interpreting his pupils' behaviour has to be brought to the realization that in each adolescent there are many people. The students – those unacademic dropouts, failure-types – who wrote for Longley showed a capacity for tenderness and kinds of nostalgia that suggest that when we categorize any pupil we also underestimate the complexity and range of his experience.* The passages which follow were written for David Longley by two sixteen-year-old members of a class of carpenters. Anyone who has worked in drama will not find them surprising, for he will know that the themes which attract adolescents are far more varied – in particular more tender, more open and more childish – than the current adolescent stereotype will admit. Adolescents are often much less eager to put away childish things than we assume.

It's Christmas Eve eight o'clock the little children are hussled up the stairs to bed. They clamber into bed their anxious clean untidyed minds vividly thinking of what the night will bring. Their eyes sweep the starlight sky looking for a bright red nose. The subconscious begin to work, do they hear bells, their heartbeat quickens, they begin to sweat with excitement. Gradually they fall asleep.

The morning has come all of a sudden the bedroom comes to life. Eager hands tear at the strong, string parcels. With great excitement their wishes becomes to live before their eyes. They gather their present in their arms and rush into their parent bedroom to show off the present which they have got.

Harvest

The work a busy cutting the wheat it is harvest time as the wheat falls hidden homes are found, the field mice run to further boundlys to make a new home, numerous birds ply to and flow garther seeds for there younger ones, once again the might machine of mankind comes along on its path of distruction and a year hard labour and

---

*This is one of the reasons why the term relevance needs to be used carefully : the tough-verse-for-tough-kids approach is misguided precisely because it is based on a superficial categorization.

growth falls to the ground. Some will survive for another year to profided the source of food for the year to come.

Personal expression of this kind is often nowadays considered the particular concern of the English teacher. It is accepted that he may use procedures which would seem eccentric in another subject and which are tolerated by his colleagues as *exceptional*. Such tolerance, however, serves only to underline the persisting assumption that, under normal circumstances, the teacher's function is not just to *instruct* but to instruct *groups*. The effects of this upon the teacher's perception of the pupils in front of him have already been suggested, but such a role has other harmful implications. It is hard not to want to 'have something to show for it all' – the syllabus worked through, novels read and ticked off, together with x pages of written work from each child. We have probably inherited guilt feelings about 'time-wasting' but our vision is further clouded, thanks largely to the organization devised by headmasters and senior staff, by the notion that assessment is one of our most sacred obligations.*
Finally, the concept of the 'successful lesson' – in which teachers are still too often trained – distracts from a proper preoccupation with the growing and learning processes taking place before their eyes. These processes, which involve particularly the adjustment of language to an increasing variety of situations and demands, and its use in developing both insight and what Richard Jones calls 'outsight'† – are too fundamental to be the concern of any individual department.

In many of these respects the primary teacher has been at an advantage. The classroom has long been for him a more fluid environment than for his secondary counterpart. In a sense too he has long been operating various kinds of what, at secondary level, is called curriculum development as part of his normal stock in trade. This should not lead us to be over-critical of developments at secondary level. Whatever its shortcomings,

*The amount of internal testing has perhaps diminshed overall but in many secondary schools teachers squander time on monthly grades, termly and yearly examinations on a scale that is by no means commensurate with the results – which in 98 per cent of cases merely confirm what was already known.

†See note on p. 145.

the current wave of curriculum innovation has one enormous potential for good; in so far as it makes consultation essential, it may dispel for ever the most pernicious educational myth of all: that a man, having qualified in his subject, knows his own business best and may safely be shut up with a class full of children, to 'get on with it', quietly, 'in his own way', for the next forty years.

The effect of this myth, and of the kinds of classroom organization it has supported, has been to encourage psychological distance and to inhibit naturalness in teacher behaviour. I have referred at various points to the way teachers are conditioned and one aspect of this is the guilt many student teachers evidently feel, against their better judgement, when they are not behaving or speaking in what they have learnt to assume is the appropriate teacherly way. There is no such way, but there are ways. As Ben Morris has pointed out* you can do things *to* children, *for* children or *with* children, though the last of these possibilities is not recognized by, for example, many contributors to Black Papers. In fact, all three kinds of activity are needed and each will have its appropriate speech style.

The student learning this is likely to make mistakes in his relationships with the class, mistakes which will be reflected in uncertainties in his language. This is not made easier for him by the fact that the children may already have expectations which reflect their own conditioning. If he adopts a matey approach they may reject it because he's not like the schoolmaster *he's supposed to be,* nor has he earned the right to be a mate. Their conception of 'schoolmasterly language' may be unduly limited, but their instinct is partly right – as long as the student is not doing the kinds of things where mateyness is natural.

In the past for many, both teacher and taught, the classroom has been a total inhibitor of the natural voice. My suggestion that modern developments in the curriculum offer some hope that this may change is borne out by the experience of those teachers who trust their intuitions, and by students too. The latter at first are uneasy when placed in close contact with small groups of children but as they work alongside them their uncer-

*The passage is quoted on p. 172.

tainties and mistakes are less remarkable than their right instincts. Most teachers and students have a 'natural' voice and it is in giving them experience above all of working *with* children that we can help them to trust it and to discover that it's quite a nice one.

4 *Language in a Developing Curriculum*

The inspector said there was much value to be got out of a navigation course even if you never got a boat. . . .

The more alterations we made in our school work, the more did it become apparent that we had done no more than make a beginning. I began to be forced back to the conclusion that there was very little in the curriculum which could defend its right to inclusion (Mackenzie, 1970).

Parliament split into two factions. The right wing pushed Latin in the school system. The left pushed science. None of them remembered us, not one had seen the problem from the inside, not one knew the struggle that your school put us through.

The men of the right were museum pieces. The Communists were laboratory mice. Both so distant from us, who cannot yet speak and who desperately need the language of today and not of yesterday – the language, not 'specializations'.

It is the language alone that makes men equal. That man is an equal who can express himself and can understand the words of others. Rich or poor, it makes no difference. But he must speak.

Leave the university, your obligations, your political parties. Start teaching right away. Start teaching the language and nothing else (School of Barbiana, 1970, p. 80).

Thus far I have sought to illustrate some of the features of the conventional school environment that are conducive to language deprivation and to show that such deprivation is frequently the result of social restriction – in the ways the pupil is encouraged to relate to both adults and to his peers. In the normal classroom, various social and emotional factors inhibit language development and consequently place limits on the learning that can take place. If I have said little about basic language skills of the kind often emphasized in 'remedial teaching' in conventional schools, this is not because such teaching is ineffective in itself, but because its potential impact is nullified by divorcing language development from the social learning with which it must go hand in hand. A number of authorities are now coming to feel that attempts to remedy linguistic deficiences have been too concerned with basic skills and not concerned enough with 'redesigning the situation at the point of performance by creating new roles, functions and communicative requirements' (Cazden, 1967).

The particular importance for the language of disadvantaged pupils of modern developments in curriculum design lies precisely in the new variety of social situations where learning is expected to take place. These situations have much in common with the facilitating speech climate of the good primary school, where the normal modes of work not only necessitate cooperative talk but also lessen the linguistic distance between the teacher and the taught. Work of the kind now frequently being tried out – involving perhaps history, geography, English and religious education, and viewing a common theme from a variety of angles – breaks down many of the assumptions that followed from the fact that each room normally contained one teacher and thirty-six pupils, and removes many of the social restraints and inhibitions upon language use that attended the archetypal instructional situation.

Many of the new situations receive official support (see, for example, Schools Council, 1970), because they have been found to increase confidence and improve motivation, as a result of which improved learning is to be expected. This is too superficial, however, though it contains some truth, and the account taken of language is inadequate. Just how far new situations and new curriculum materials lead to improved learning will depend on the opportunities created for an extended variety of language experience. Where schemes have been particularly successful one may justifiably infer that this is partly because the materials are relevant and interesting and are used under a stimulating variety of working conditions. Such variety may rouse interest; I doubt whether it can of itself *sustain* the motivation upon which learning depends. The crucial factor is not even the diversity of social situations in which the pupils work – individually, in pairs, small groups, large groups. It is true that much of the teacher's success in these conditions will depend upon his ability to adapt his role to the particular situation. More vital still, however, is his ability to use both the new teaching materials and his own new flexibility of role to create contexts in which pupils are motivated to explore an extended range of language functions. It is in so far as they facilitate such provision that we may best evaluate either the procedures of an individual teacher or the potential advantages of a new curriculum; the quality of learning depends upon it.

The application of such a criterion remains uncommon. It is true that most recent reports contain some general statement about the importance of language and may even make a passing obeisance to Bernstein, but they pay little further attention to the topic even when they are considering new developments in the curriculum; the Plowden Report (Vol. I, p. 495) for example, devotes three paragraphs to *speech*, placing these predictably and significantly in the section on 'English'. Official attention in general prefers to concentrate upon materials, methodology and organization. 'Themes', 'interdisciplinary inquiry', discussion groups, and team-teaching are advocated in ways which ignore the dynamics of the class or group and show inadequate understanding both of the role of language and the actual or potential impact of new methods upon language use. We are left in no doubt that inquiry-based activity, project and discovery methods are approved, but their distinctive features remain obscure and one rarely sees, for example, inquiry methods related to the kind of considerations raised by Postman and Weingartner (see ch. 3 p. 25).

Curriculum changes at secondary level are in fact not widely understood. Even those who have grasped that the new schemes represent, in large part, efforts to meet some foreseeable consequences of the raising of the school-leaving age may not realize the extent to which we are still digesting the implications of the 1944 Act – of secondary education for all.

The cynic might say that curriculum development was forced on schools by the fear of what might ensue if we kept adolescents waiting there for a further year. Certainly there has been a tendency to think too narrowly in terms of 'something to do in the extra year', though many schools that have grappled with the problem have quickly become convinced of the need to plan for a two-year programme. Even this may not be enough; it is no good trying, in the last years, to graft an outgoing, interdisciplinary programme on to a curriculum which for the first three or four years has been relatively traditional. Several new schemes make assumptions which take too little account of the conditioning already undergone by the less able pupils in particular. As one recent report emphasized (Schools Council, 1970), the problem is not that they leave school at fifteen or sixteen, but that *as far as school learning goes* they 'leave' school at the age of about twelve!

To suggest that the redesigning of the curriculum has been held back by an underemphasis on language is not to deny the importance of some changes that have taken place, nor to suggest that they have no sound theoretical basis. The significance of changes in the role of the teacher has already been emphasized, but other positive aspects demand consideration. Changes in the secondary curriculum may have been hastened by the spectres of thousands more bored adolescents staying on at school, but we must also recognize that many authors of curriculum schemes have been consistently motivated by the need to invest school work with new meaning – *to make it real*, or *relevant*. Here Sybil Marshall's comments, from her evidence to the Walsall Seminar, raise the most important issues:

'Start from where the child is' is a good motto. But what *is* the child? Start from where his body is, with environmental studies that ought to be renamed 'local studies' to prevent misunderstanding, or from where his mind is (probably on the row his mum and dad had last night), or from where his imagination, his 'shaping spirit' is? I have never had much patience with the school of thought that desires a child from a coalmining village to study coal mines, or the village child to give weeks of its time and attention to the work of the parish pump. The real child is often where his daydreams are.

There is of course some ground for believing that, for the English pupil in a rural area, village pumps may be of more immediate interest than, for example, ocean currents round Japan but this should not lead us to see relevance in mere proximity. There are, moreover, aspects of Japanese life and history which, like myth and literature, may feed the pupil's imagination. Relevance is not automatically inherent in any subject but is latent in most teaching situations. Those who have taken the opposite, simplistic, view have tended to replace traditional curriculum content with other content which may be, at worst, only a shade less arbitrary. Studies of the village pump may be of two kinds – open or closed. Many modish failures to interest kids in their own backyards can be attributed to the teacher's presumption; whatever the potential interest of the topic, this has been killed because the pupil has received the message – it may even be explicit – that he *ought* to be interested in it. Such a message clearly implies that 'teacher knows' and the pupil, with not even a backyard to call his own, refuses to play this new game. It has become no more and no less interesting than any other topic in which both the content *and also the child's perception of it* have been prescribed in advance; all are unreal.

A classic instance of this closed approach is found in *Society and the Young School Leaver* (Schools Council, 1967, p. 64). This is not a description of work actually done but a suggested *model* for the systematic exploration of the environment, called 'The 97 Bus'. That it is systematic – above all else – emerges clearly from the layout; the purposes of the 'inquiry', for example:

(i) To help the pupils to become familiar with the district where they live, and to appreciate some of the benefits and problems of their own locality.
(ii) To illustrate a local public transport route through the people working it and using it.
(iii) To bring forward for discussion the differences between public and private transport.
(iv) To use a variety of techniques such as interviews with special people, social surveys, discussions and field studies into environment and local history through local records.
(v) To bring out other social problems, e.g. of conveying people to work, shops and entertainment centres.

After a general glance at 'the method of the inquiry' and discussion of the making and use of a film as what is coyly termed a 'point of departure', there comes the central section which details a series of tasks:

As the emphasis is through persons and personalities, most of the assignments will be of the interview type. Therefore it is important that the boys and girls have some training in interview techniques, and also that the people to be interviewed have agreed to help with the inquiry. These assignments are for two people together rather than individuals and they are based on an actual bus journey which was investigated on these lines by a school in Kent. The bus passes the school on its way from the neighbouring town to another town thirty miles away. Many of the boys and girls use the bus to and from school. None had made the whole journey. It is a typical cross-country route which moves from orchard and hop-growing country to a pastoral sheep-raising area. Within a mile of the school is a large village where many of the children live.

Pair 1 will board the bus at its starting point at 9.00 a.m. making the complete journey (1½ hours), recording at each stop the number of people (men, women, children) boarding and leaving, and if possible recording the length of the journey each makes. They will try to assess the purpose of the journey, in simple terms: going to work, going to school, going to hospital, going to shop. This pair will return on the same bus repeating the observations.

Pair 2 will repeat this journey starting at 1.30 p.m.

Pair 3 will travel on the top of the bus and record the view – describing the nature of the country, the farming, the houses and the traffic *en route*. Simple categories will be suggested, e.g. large, medium, small, tiny, for the houses. This pair will need a large-scale map to which they can refer their observations.

Pair 4 will take the school camera and at points previously agreed with Pair 3 will take photographs to illustrate the observations made by Pair 3.

Colour transparency 35 mm film will be used.

Thirteen assignments are listed in this way, the thirteenth pair being required to 'talk to some of the bus drivers and learn as much as they can about good driving, road courtesy and dangerous actions by motorists, cyclists and pedestrians which lead to accidents'. This is by no means all. The example has further sections on using outside speakers, on extra projects and concludes with suggestions about the final outcome:

Presentation: The exhibition at the end of this area of inquiry will be able to show some or all of these items:

1. Public transport is a vital part of the urban and rural scene.
2. Many different kinds of travellers depend upon the 97 bus.

3. As well as travellers, the jobs of many people (drivers, conductors, maintenance men, cleaners, traffic superintendents, office staff) depend upon this bus.

4. The impact of the 97 bus on local traffic, police, industry, shopping and entertainment.

5. The way local history and geography is reflected in the vast changes in public transport in the last hundred years.

6. Transport in other areas, not only in England, but all over the world.

7. Public transport depends on people (sometimes immigrants) and we depend on public transport for both work and leisure.

This scheme has been widely criticized: it is so structured, so teacher-directed, so fact-dominated as to make a mockery of the term 'inquiry' – who, we may ask, *wants to know*? One may marvel at the claim made at one point that 'The nature of the inquiry lends itself to direct involvement and personal experience.' It could be argued that sustained boredom is a personal experience, but hardly that it promotes the involvement needed for such experience to be educative. All this is not to suggest that the scheme should be consigned to oblivion, however. It is worth remembering because it exhibits common weaknesses in an extreme form, because of its mixture of insight and misapprehension. On the positive side, it is an attempt to 'start from where the child is'; the topic has *potential* relevance. More than this there is the recognition that pupils may gain from contact with the community at large. The crucial flaw, however, lies less in the failure to see the possibilities for language growth afforded by such contact – serious though that is – than in the whole approach to the topic. The teacher has presumed to make the pupil's territory his own and in so doing has made it unreal; in such a 'closed' treatment the environment is not brought into school, it becomes part of it.

Before considering what is needed to make relevance real, I should like to look at another example from the same source (Schools Council, 1967, p. 23). This is another, more representative scheme which also attempts to start from where the child is. It describes work with about a hundred third- and fourth-year pupils in an old, mixed secondary modern school in a depressed area; eight teachers were involved and about a third of the week given over to the scheme.

Project Scheme
Theme: 'Myself and the World'

Theme to be subdivided into three parts:

(a) 'Myself'
(b) 'My fellows'
(c) 'My environment'

Though the time allocated to each section will of necessity be fluid, it is proposed to attempt to use the above headings in three consecutive school terms:

1. Autumn term – 'Myself'
2. Spring term – 'My fellows'
3. Summer term – 'My environment'

In the second year, the third heading will be the basis of further study, advancing from the child's immediate surroundings, in ever expanding circles, to all parts of the world.

Our present concern is with the first term's work. The emphasis here will be, not only on 'Myself', as a topic, but also upon 'individual work', in the pursuit of this theme. It is suggested that the groups will pursue this aim as follows:

(a) Scientific group	1. Anatomy and physiology	'What I am as a physical being.'
	2. General science	'What I need scientifically analysed.'
(b) Liberal-studies group	1. Psychological and moral	'What I am mentally, emotionally and spiritually.'
	2. Projection	'Discovery of myself through drama.'
(c) Social-studies group	1. Economic	'What I need economically.'
	2. Historical	'My heritage' – the development of man's needs through the ages.
(d) Technical group	1. Woodwork 2. Metalwork 3. Domestic science 4. Needlework	'What I can do – development of my own manual skills.'

The content of the schemes for the individual groups will be devised jointly by discussion and cooperation amongst the members of staff concerned so that points of contact in the work contemplated may be clearly established.

This outline – it is only the index to a scheme that runs to twenty pages – seems worth quoting in the first instance because it is based on that kind of self-questioning by the staff that must precede the design of effective curricula:

When the study group met initially, to consider the best method of education for this large group of the school population, we were faced with a number of questions which had to be answered before any scheme could be devised.

1. What are the needs of these children in the present and the future?
2. How can learning be made a live and interesting occupation to their minds?
3. How can one overcome subject prejudices?
4. How can constructive criticism be encouraged when surveying the world around them?

In its scope and its attempt to be relevant, this scheme is similar to much work now going on in secondary schools. It would appear to offer pupils considerable opportunity to utilize their own experience instead of playing the old secondary-school game of pretending they've never had any (nothing relevant to the school's academic purposes, that is). More particularly, such a scheme provides opportunities for language development: at the simplest level one can hardly have pupils working at this particular topic without *depending* on their frequent personal contributions to an extent quite different from anything in the old curriculum. The scheme also clearly depends on the staff's willingness to encourage more flexible and varied working relationships within the classroom. The staff will have to do some things which are surprisingly 'unteacherly' and novel enough to encourage language use in a way uninhibited by the adoption of stereotyped teacher–pupil roles. The pupil knows more about himself than the teacher does, for example, and hence the authority has shifted, only temporarily, perhaps, but significantly. The content of the course and the social educational situations it implies may both be expected to have a positive effect upon confidence and motivation. On the basis of the evidence set out in chapter two we seem justified in looking for a consequent improvement in language.

The impression given by this outline – especially in the attention to the predicament and needs of non-academic adolescents – is of a much more open approach. It doesn't much matter whether this is a true impression (had the scheme been presented in full it might have seemed quite different) the point I want to stress is that for 'relevance', for starting from where the pupils are, to mean anything, topics must be treated in ways that leave some room for pupil initiative, so that the outcomes are not predestined. If I really start from where the child is this implies a considerable degree of acceptance, openness and flexibility on my part.

Openness has already been referred to in discussing class control but the issue is much wider than that. Openness may be an aspect of the teacher's relation to his subject matter, as well as to his pupils. It may also describe the relationship between the school and the surrounding community.

To take this last point first, the best single indication of the school's attitude to the community it exists to serve lies in its attitude to parents. At primary level, schools have become steadily more accessible in recent years in a way beneficial to both teacher and parent. Parents now have a much better appreciation of the teacher's role as 'resource person' – setting up a learning environment – as well as 'instructor'. At secondary level things have not greatly changed. There have admittedly been some schools with exceptional policies towards parents but the traditional tendency to resist 'outside interference' remains dominant. Parents have come to accept that they are welcome, once or twice a year, to visit the school to discuss the progress of their offspring. It is equally clearly not within their province to question the way those offspring are taught, the assumption being that failure is due to *their* not *learning* what the staff have *taught*. In *Teaching as a Subversive Activity* a vivid attack on this kind of attitude is made by Neil Postman and Charles Weingartner, querying our reaction if a salesman were to tell us, 'I sold it him, but he didn't buy it.' The situation is not peculiar to England and America, however, as the Italian peasant boys who wrote *Letter to a Teacher* make clear:

The poorest among the parents don't do a thing. They don't even suspect what is going on. . . . In their time, up in the country, they left school at nine.

If things are not going so well, it must be that their child is not cut out for studying. 'Even the teacher said so. A real gentleman. He asked me to sit down. He showed me the record book. And a test all covered with red marks. I suppose we just weren't blessed with an intelligent boy. He will go to work in the fields, like us' (School of Barbiana, 1970, p. 34).

The tendency of some teachers to treat parents as peasants is more germane to the issue of curriculum innovation than it seems; such treatment is hardly compatible with the acceptance and openness needed to motivate learning, to revive interest in bored, deprived adolescents. A study of new curricula leaves one uncertain how far basic attitudes, to subject matter as well as to pupils, have changed. Approaches to a 'relevant' topic like *The Family* may suggest merely old wine in new bottles, for example:

Basically the work was divided into two main time approaches:

1. The structure, function and purpose of the family in:
(a) Tribal situation
(b) Middle Ages
(c) Industrial Revolution
(d) The early twentieth century

2. The changes, and reasons for these changes, in the family since grandfather.
(a) External influence:
   i Industrial expansion
   ii Communications (cars, roads, mass media)
   iii Spending patterns and wages
   iv The welfare state
   v Education
(b) Effect of 2(a) on the internal structure of the family with particular reference to:
   i Women at work
   ii Early marriage
   iii Decline in authority of 'father'
   iv Teenage culture

The layout of schemes like that from which this extract is taken often appears to overemphasize both structure and factual learning and suggests that some teachers have not come to terms with the need to adopt new roles and a wider range of objectives. Everyday observation would offer strong support to such an inference but it is almost impossible to judge from any single outline – even if quoted *in toto** – how far such apparent rigidity fairly reflects the attitudes and procedures among the teachers who carried it out.

This difficulty derives in part from the nature of the process by which new developments are disseminated. By the time the report of the original observer – in itself, even at first, incomplete and tending to fix on only some of the essential features – has been discussed in various meetings, compared with similar reports, and finally edited in order to fit in with specifications for publication – to put it mildly, something has been lost. A second process of over-simplification follows publication, for now it becomes the topic of educational gossip in which a convenient but misleading kind of shorthand is necessary. This means that distinctive but not necessarily the most significant features of a scheme are used to label it. The result is a half-informed audience who are aware that projects, or themes, or interdisciplinary work, or team teaching are important but are unsure of what precisely each term involves.

I do not wish to lay the blame on bodies like the Schools Council for inefficient dissemination. Given that the medium is the printed word, weaknesses are inevitable. Here again, the medium is the message: my reception of the 'content' is partly determined by the fact that it's in an official publication or uses emotive labels like 'project' or 'involvement'. I may be led by a neat tabulation to see logical connections where none in fact exist, or where they *need* not exist. Above all the editing of such schemes for publication tends to lead to their presentation in a form which overemphasizes content simply because the easiest thing to transmit is a list of topics dealt with, or of things done.

*The whole scheme is included in an appendix, so that the reader may be able to form his own conclusions. It forms in any case an interesting contrast with the Nuffield/Schools Council Humanities Project.

The fact that we lack information necessary for the evaluation of particular schemes need not however blind us to the possible dangers. Some of these – relating to the teachers' attitudes both to the pupils and to the material to be taught – have been mentioned already. A further grave danger attends the more elaborate schemes like the last one quoted, which depended upon team teaching. Elaboration of this type inevitably entails an organizational and material investment by the school that is all too often at odds with flexibility and openness, however potentially relevant the themes and topics may appear. Interdisciplinary inquiry demands that we attend to the links between subjects, but the more teachers and pupils involved, the greater the tendency for these to become rigid. The idea of one main theme per term has an exquisite but treacherous simplicity. Was there, one wonders, anything more unnatural than this in the old textbound curriculum – how long does it take to batter a relevant theme into irrelevance? Finding themes and compiling material – to say nothing of organizing the courses that ensue – may so easily distract attention from the learning processes (as opposed to *products*) that should be our primary concern. I recall a headmaster who announced to me, with evident satisfaction, that the second-year pupils would be doing interdisciplinary work, *all the following term,* on the theme of *change*. At such moments it is hard to suppress the conviction that thinking stops once a theme has been discovered and the timetable problems overcome.

I have argued that for material to be in any real sense relevant to the pupil, the teacher's approach to both needs to be characterized by acceptance, flexibility and openness. For years now work in schools has offered increasing opportunities for contact with the community at large. The importance of this in terms of language development can hardly be overemphasized, but the extent to which the pupils benefit will depend upon the teacher's ability to set up situations which make demands on him yet leave him room to use his own initiative. It is possible to take a group of adolescents on a week-long excursion into a totally new environment and to transform the whole thing into yet another 'lesson'. R. F. Mackenzie, a pioneer in the extensive use of such excursions for children from a depressed area in the Scottish coalfields, discovered that 'the least successful (teachers) were those who had prepared a scheme of work and were determined to see it through.' The roots of success were, however, less easy to identify:

The most successful was a girl of twenty-one, an uncertificated teacher. When she and her group returned, I asked if she would write a report. She said reluctantly that she would. A few days later I said, 'What about this report?'

She replied, 'I've been thinking about it, but really we didn't do very much.'

'What did you do?'

'Sat around and talked, mostly. Sometimes we didn't even talk' (Mackenzie, 1970).

The apparent inactivity that puzzled this teacher would have been a source of anxiety or guilt in one less secure; to be open in the way she was requires a faith in the pupils. The teacher also needs to be secure in the knowledge that a situation where nothing 'teacherly' is happening is not necessarily an educational vacuum. This should become clearer in the second part of this chapter, when we shall look in detail at some classrooms, but it may be helpful at this point to see what openness in a conventional setting (a science lesson) looks like.

One day while he was, like an orthodox teacher, following the scheme of work which gave one lesson to filling and melting glass tubing, he discovered that his pupils had suddenly become absorbed in what they were doing – melting glass, pulling it out like chewing gum, experimenting happily in making shapes. Instead of stopping them and saying, 'Now let's be finished with play and get on with science', he suddenly realized that *this was science*. The children were absorbed with the plasticity of melted glass; they were conducting their own inquiries into the nature of things. This was science, the teacher said, because there was within it the delight of the artist and the curiosity of the child (Mackenzie, 1970, p. 23).

If the organization of complex interdisciplinary schemes makes this kind of openness less feasible, we may well consider whether the attendant losses outweigh the gains. Mackenzie adds a footnote to the above account which is suggestive –

it seemed to me significant that when I mentioned this incident to the art teacher, he, too, decided to give his pupils the opportunity to mould shapes out of melted glass tubing, providing them with a new medium in which to give reality to their dreams and imaginings.

A very modest instance of cross-fertilization this, but I suspect that some of the most fruitful cooperative enterprises have similar origins. A staffroom climate that facilitates the interchange of such ideas may be more effective than cooperation institutionalized (and ossified) within the timetable.

Not all schemes have the same weaknesses, however, and I should like to mention two that are markedly different from those mentioned so far. The first, the Humanities Curriculum Project, sponsored jointly by the Schools Council and the Nuffield Foundation, is intended 'for use with fourteen to sixteen year olds of average or below average ability and can either be used as a separate "subject" on the timetable or as a core for the integration of traditional subjects'.*

The first feature that distinguishes this project from schemes already mentioned is its special function, which is made clear by the terms of reference given when the Humanities Curriculum Development Project was started:

To offer to schools and to teachers such stimulus, support and materials as may be appropriate to the mounting, as an element in education, of inquiry-based courses which cross the subject boundaries between English, history, geography, religious studies and social studies (Stenhouse, 1968).

Though it offers some suggestions about the structure that could underlie work in each 'area of inquiry', the Project leaves the detailed planning and organization to the individual schools concerned. The Project's main outcome has been the provision of materials, collected under major themes. While the subjects (for example, *The Family, War and Society, Poverty*) are in no way remarkable, the quantity of material offered for each theme is unprecedented in this country: reproductions of paintings and photographs, cuttings from all kinds of newspapers

*Accounts of the Project may be found in the *Journal of Curriculum Studies*, vol. 1, no. 1, 1968; *New Society*, 24 July 1969 and *The Humanities Curriculum Project: Interim Report*, 1969, Schools Council Publications Company. See also *The Humanities Project: An Introduction*, Heinemann, a copy of which is supplied with each pack.

and periodicals, extracts from books – all these in the form of separate broadsheets; in addition to which there are colour slides, tape-recordings and film. Each 'area of inquiry' has its own teacher's handbook, but this is concise and leaves the teacher free to arrange the material more or less as he desires, though it offers some hints – perhaps for those who find the whole thing overwhelming (as some do).

In one major particular, however – the second distinctive feature of the project – it goes beyond the provision of resources and seeks to affect teaching procedures: within the context of the use of its material, it proposes a modification of the teacher's role. He is to renounce the assumption of authority in favour of a function which is neutral and procedural. This is particularly important in view of the project's deliberate emphasis upon controversial material. Whether one accepts this emphasis as helpful or essential in such a scheme or not, the reasoning behind the demand that the teacher should modify his procedures appears well-founded:

To justify neutrality and impartiality in practical educational terms one has to consider what goes on in a classroom. The chairman of a discussion, if he is not careful, breaches his neutrality by a series of small intrusions on points of detail. He may say 'Yes' or 'A good point', and thus endorse a particular point of view. He may ask leading questions: 'Don't you feel that dropping the atomic bomb on Hiroshima was morally wrong?' or 'Do you think that people who have "done wrong" are bound to be afraid of contracting VD?' or 'Do you think it's unnatural to live in cities?'

Our study of tape-recordings of class discussion shows clearly that such leading questions and confirmatory responses from the chairman-teacher destroy a discussion by redirecting it from an attempt to understand the issue involved into a guessing game about the mind of the teacher. A 'guessing game' is merely disguised instruction. Neutral chairmanship is thus not only a professional ethic in controversial matters but also the means to put responsibility on the pupils in the task of gaining understanding (Stenhouse, 1969).

It is reassuring to find insights of this kind in a curriculum scheme; moreover the points made about classroom dynamics are clearly in line with the general argument about in-school language deprivation that I have tried to put forward. It is therefore not surprising to learn that the aspect of the project that has been most commonly objected to, or misunderstood, is the emphasis upon the teacher's new role, as a neutral chairman. At first sight this conception appears to encourage that openness on which I have laid stress, and the teacher's unwillingness to adopt such a role – a source of recurrent complaint among project organizers – to be further evidence of inflexibility. Clearly some teachers *are* inflexible but I suspect that others have renounced neutrality because they have found that to treat controversial subjects in this way, consistently, is *unnatural* – leading to a new kind of inflexibility. In this context, though the issue is not quite the same, Kohl's remarks on what openness is, and is not, may be illuminating:

It is important not to equate an open classroom with a 'permissive environment'. In an open classroom the teacher *must be as much himself as the pupils are themselves*. This means that if the teacher is angry he ought to express his anger, and if he is annoyed at someone's behaviour he ought to express that, too. In an authoritarian classroom annoying behaviour is legislated out of existence. In a 'permissive' classroom the teacher pretends it isn't annoying. He also permits students to behave only in certain ways, thereby retaining the authority over their behaviour he pretends to be giving up. In an open situation the teacher tries to express what he feels and to deal with each situation as a communal problem (Kohl, 1969, p. 15, my italics).

The teacher who has been unhappy in a situation in which he has not felt free to be himself may have misunderstood the intention of the scheme, which is to prevent teachers from *forcing* their opinions rather than from declaring them, but early explanations of neutrality were probably both over-dogmatic and under-illustrated. More importantly, the teacher's discomfort in his new role may reflect a keener awareness of his pupils than he has been given credit for. It is true that the article by Stenhouse from which I quoted stresses the need to ensure that the pupils know the conventions of the new situation and feel secure enough to contribute. But how does one *ensure* this, and how long does the process take? Some children – those who already command an extensive language repertoire – will find no difficulty in adapting, but it was not for them that the scheme was devised. Where teachers refuse to play the game (and we should face the fact that it is still a game in the child's eyes) according to the new rules, it is oversimplifying to see the refusal merely as further proof of the way their minds have been conditioned. Some at least may do so because they recognize the extent to which the minds and responses of the pupils have suffered the same fate. To work in the way Stenhouse suggests is feasible but demands a curriculum that has been moving *in this direction* for two or three years.

Teachers may also be right to have reservations about such a heavy emphasis upon large group-discussion situations.* Quite apart from the ways in which the school curriculum in the earlier years (to say nothing of teaching procedures) may have failed to prepare pupils of average and below average ability for such situations, all the evidence we have considered so far would suggest that the large group discussion – however it is 'chaired' – is not going to be an easy one for many children. In chapter two (p. 61) I noted Sidney Bolt's reservations about some of the most popular discussion topics, whose controversial nature (a desirable feature in Stenhouse's eyes) is more likely to elicit voting postures than close and searching discussion. According to Bolt, such discussion is more likely to arise from the study of literary texts, which stimulate by their particularity. At first sight, the Humanities Project might seem to meet his requirements since it provides a wealth of material that is highly concrete and particular, and indeed lays an emphasis which he might approve on the proper use of evidence. The teacher of English may be critical of the very small proportion of explicitly literary items, but it can be argued that it was not conceived as a literary course.

Such an answer is not entirely satisfactory, however. Whether or not the literary text can do all that Bolt claimed, the items in the Humanities pack must fulfil an analogous function. Given the neutral role of the teacher, the success of the scheme must depend on the capacity of the items not merely to *provoke* but to *sustain* discussion. Here we may find a further explanation of teachers' tendency to 'misuse' material, a significant proportion of which is too abstract and too generalized for the

*The recommended maximum size is about fifteen. This itself is large, and in practice it seems quite common for whole classes to be involved.

ability range for which it was designed.* This difficulty is foreseen; in the introductory notes to the handbook on *The Family* we read:

The material in the collection now offered has been selected from a very large amount with an attempt to provide as wide a range of opinion and experience as possible at a level which most pupils will be able to apprehend, if not fully comprehend.

The distinction is a nice one, perhaps, but from the point of view of the teacher working with a bored and bemused group of unacademic adolescents it is not much help.

In such a predicament, the teacher may follow the warning about the inadvisability of 'working one's way steadily through the collection as if it were a textbook', and ignore some of the most difficult passages. Though he is clearly meant to use his own discretion, however, it is hard for him to be ruthless enough. The package in itself inexorably conveys the message that it is there, in some way, to be *done* and it may be hard for the teacher to escape from guilt-feeling about not using all this wealth of material to the best advantage. If you present a teacher with a package of 250 items (to say nothing of additional film and tape material), there is the further risk that he will be so preoccupied with the manipulation of these staggering resources that he loses sight of the class altogether. When you invite him *at the same time* to alter his procedures quite radically – whether or not such alteration be justified – you place an additional burden upon him.

If I have laboured these points of criticism, this is because the project is of unusual importance and likely to exert a great influence. I fancy however that one can detect here a disparity between the quality and potential of the materials offered and of the supporting theory, which is a price one has to pay when research projects are subjected to a pressure to produce curriculum materials that is becoming all too common.† This is all the

*The amount of potentially difficult material will be apparent from a glance at two typical pages of the synopsis, reproduced in Appendix 2, where the introductory notes are also reproduced in full (p. 186).

†But fortunately not universal. Early work on the Schools Council Curriculum Study, *The Arts and the Adolescent,* is remarkable; it is based on close analysis of classroom situations and on the establishment of a vocabulary with which teachers can talk about them.

more disappointing in a scheme which appeared to be based on the importance of children talking. The insights into classroom and language seem, in the end, to be no more than half-truths, likely to lead to new kinds of inflexibility. In more than one school I know, the teachers' inability to make sense of the stipulated procedures (together with a natural conscientiousness) has led to the material becoming not much more than a mammoth comprehension course.

Whereas the Humanities Project emphasized the spoken language in ways which largely presupposed some reorganization of the curriculum, the last scheme I want to consider makes no structural changes and places the emphasis upon literacy – as opposed to 'oracy'. *Hooked on Books,* Daniel Fader and E. B. McNeil (1969), describes how Fader came to redesign the English curriculum in the American equivalent of one of our Borstal institutions. Having worked hitherto with university students in an academic department, he came to the problem ignorant but also blessedly fresh. After extensive observation of English teaching in schools, he produced an analysis of the problems and made suggestions. These were so simple and logical that some distrusted them, particularly where they felt themselves and their methods the objects of scathing comment. Poor performance in English, Fader's observation told him, was the product of irrelevance of material and mishandling of the child. Because the material was irrelevant, and the demands for literacy were restricted to the English classroom, the student 'put his mind out to lunch' during the five periods; he was less often a 'can't reader' than a 'won't reader'. The mishandling was seen in the fact that whenever Fader asked to see a school's best teacher of unacademic children (potential or inevitable dropouts) he was invariably shown the best 'warder'. The children such warders supervise, he notes, are often in the USA called 'terminal' students, 'a word borrowed from the vocabulary of death by teachers who recognize their true vocations'.

Fader's strategy was simple. Firstly he sought to make it impossible for students to evade the demands to read and to write. Being realists, he argued, they would find it uncomfortable to resist for more than a proportion of the time: if the demand came in every lesson they would submit. And they did.

The second part of his policy was based on the conviction that most adolescents were only too conscious of their lack of word-power and that given favourable circumstances they would work to acquire skills that the society around them so evidently valued. The answer here was the provision of enormous quant-itites of reading material, most of it apparently 'uneducational', often in magazine or paperback form, to be available in *every* class. Thirdly, he recognized that the child could learn to value language in a more personal, even private way; to this end students had to write two pages per week in a 'journal' – two pages which were not marked, just ticked off when written and which could be about anything. He notes their disbelief when they discovered that they were free even to *copy* in order to fulfil their quota, and goes on to describe the way in which the journal became a valued outlet.

Such seem to me the major features of Fader's programme. The style of some of the suggestions in the book may make an English reader impatient; he may be sceptical about the evidence of the programme's success. Certainly the programme is deficient in the place it assigns to the spoken word, as Fader himself now recognizes. These weaknesses seem unimportant compared with the achievement: the presentation of a method whereby a *concerted* language policy may be evolved by an English teacher working with his colleagues in other disciplines.

As well as the diffused emphasis on literacy, the organization of the scheme is interesting: unlike many other schemes, which involve some restructuring of the curriculum, this accepts a relatively conventional framework but transforms it. Fader reports that teachers of other subjects were at first predictably unwilling to sacrifice their valuable time to English. However a striking proportion of those who gave the scheme a chance became convinced of the benefit, not merely in general terms of proficiency in English, but specifically *in terms of improved learning within their own subject fields.*

The weakness of most curriculum development work is sim-ply that it doesn't really face the question – raised by the quota-tions at the head of this chapter – is *anything* more important than language? The Fader programme at least gets close to an answer and does so in a way that does not distract the teacher by an overemphasis on new content or organization. I have argued that we need to pay much closer attention not merely to language but to the range of uses to which language is put, an idea which is not explicit in many new curricula. Thus there are dangers of our repeating the old mistakes, replacing the restrictiveness of the authoritarian instructional mode by that of Stenhouse's neutral chairman, for example. The foundation upon which we ought to build is a proper consideration of the purposes which language serves. As Professor Halliday put it:

Our conception of language, if it is to be adequate for meeting the needs of the child, will need to be exhaustive. It must incorporate all the child's own 'models', to take account of the varied demands on language that he himself makes. The child's understanding of what language is is derived from his own experience of language in situations of use. . . .

Let us summarize the models in terms of the child's intentions, since different uses of language may be seen as realizing different intentions. In its instrumental function, language is used for the satisfaction of material needs; this is the 'I want' function. The regulatory is the 'do as I tell you' function, language in the control of behaviour. The interactional function is that of getting along with others, the 'me and him' function (including 'me and my mummy'). The personal is related to this: it is the expression of identity, of the self, which develops largely *through* linguistic interaction; the 'here I come' function, perhaps. The heuristic is the use of language to learn, to explore reality: the function of 'tell me why', the imaginative is that of 'let's pretend', whereby the reality is created, and what is being explored is the child's own mind, including language itself. The representational is the 'I've got something to tell you' function, that of the communication of content.

What we have called 'models' are the images that we have for language arising out of these functions. Language is 'defined' for the child by its uses; it is something that serves this set of needs (Halliday, 1969).

It is worth noting that Professor Halliday's paper is called '*Relevant models of language*'. To provide classroom situations that enable the child to explore the uses of language is to go a long way towards giving him an education that is indeed *relevant*. In the next section, I shall look at work in classrooms that is specific enough to shed new light on the themes in the first part of this chapter, and to suggest some opportunities that curriculum designers still tend to overlook.

Despite the general criticisms already made the importance of changes in the way the curriculum is organized may lie less in the changes themselves than in the fact that they compel teachers to modify their procedures quite substantially. It seems unlikely that a more theoretical approach to curriculum content would have had comparable effects, though one cannot be happy about a situation where improvements in language, and hence in learning, are largely fortuitous. Our hope must be that the first wave of curriculum development will prepare the way for a more intense scrutiny of what teachers are about. In such a second stage, groups of teachers who had learnt to work together on interdisciplinary themes might devote themselves to the study of skills. Teachers examining a concept such as *comprehension,* for example, might discover its different interpretation by different specialisms. This would force them to look at more specific skills, and also to decide which should have priority, at what age or ability level, in which area of study. Are there times when we may be satisfied with a vague 'awareness', or do we require a positive response by the pupil? If so, how personal and individual may this be – would a poem be an acceptable response from a pupil engaged in a geographical study of a strand-line, for example? If this is not 'factual' enough, are we rejecting it in favour of a response which makes a fumbling attempt to replicate our own perceptions? We may of course want not fact but something like *guesswork,* and the place of deduction and inference may be usefully discussed with colleagues in other disciplines.

This example serves to emphasize the extent to which thinking about teaching objectives means thinking about *language in context*. We cannot long engage in such study, however, without facing the importance of objectives which have more to do with social behaviour than with conventional academic aims. The implications of this are suggested in another article by Professor Halliday:

Language is a form of culturally determined behaviour and this behaviour includes the ability to take on a range of linguistically defined roles in speech situations. Unless the child grows up in an environment in which all these speech situation roles are open to him, he will fail to master important areas in the grammar of his language. Therefore, he must be given the opportunity to behave linguistically in all the culturally determined roles which the language recognizes: to ask and answer questions, to give and respond to commands, to explain things, to express reservations, contradictions, contrasts; to vary the key of his utterances; to explore, in other words, a full range of linguistic relations with his interlocutors. It is no doubt largely because the nursery school provides the opportunity for the child to explore, and to switch among, his linguistic roles that it can make the essential difference between educational success and failure for the child when he goes into the school system. The child has to learn not only to perform in all these roles but also to respond to and identify correctly the roles of others; this is part of the socialization process (Halliday, 1968).

It is largely because of its recognition of such objectives, and the way this supports the individual teacher at a time when he is subject to many and confusing pressures, that I want to look in this section at some situations in the work of the English Department under George Robertson* at Abbey Wood Comprehensive School. The fact that the classes described are unstreamed does not mean that the principles and methods are inappropriate or unworkable in more conventional, streamed, situations – indeed the opposite is probably true.

Though what I saw at Abbey Wood was chiefly interesting because of the way language learning and socialization went hand in hand, it also shed light upon several concepts we have just been considering – 'openness' and 'relevance', for example. At the same time, it showed some of the language possibilities latent in schemes that I have criticized. The work of Robertson and his colleagues will also serve to make meaningful the concept of the teacher as a 'resource person'. In all these respects, it is probably less significant that the illustrations are drawn from work in an *English* department, than that they reflect a climate in which department staff consistently engaged in discussion and pooling of ideas – in other words a department where a concerted language policy was a feasibility. A truly

* Now headmaster, Tavistock Boys' School, Croydon.

professional sharing of ideas does more than support the teacher; it enables him to find difficult teaching situations a source of stimulation as well as of anxiety. Some of the most penetrating recent thinking about language – the work of Bernstein is an example – has arisen from reflection about similarly taxing predicaments. Within a school department, however, talk among colleagues is not enough. In a large school particularly, any policy is likely to provoke some resistance, no matter how it is formulated. The only way to modify the professional behaviour of the reactionary and the self-deluder is to let them see *in successful operation* some of those ideas they find surprising or unconvincing.

There remains one reason for citing this work which has a good deal to do with its source in an English department, though this entails no serious limitation of its relevance. There has been an increasing concern, in English studies, with the adolescent's sense of identity; one aspect of this is the emphasis upon what is often loosely called 'creative' work, but it is not the only one. It would be as silly, however, to assume that this concern is the proper monopoly of the English department, as to assume that kids only use language in English periods. The adolescent's search for identity matters to all who attempt to teach him:

The social skill to be learned during this period, and it is very much a *social* skill, is to be one's self, to stand for and against things consistently and expressly, in ways that make one recognizedly one's own man, in private and in public.

This quotation, from Richard Jones's *Fantasy and Feeling in Education* (1968), is not just a topical, permissive, beatitude – Blessed is he who does his own thing – but a statement of fundamental importance where the teaching of adolescents is concerned. It does not imply that 'practical teaching' has been left behind; but it does mean that the practicalities are impracticable until this has been attended to.

One grasps one's own identity largely through language and the situations in which it is used. In various schools, or parts of one school, the adolescent may receive partial answers to his unspoken but urgent question, 'Who am I?' Where these are of the kind that teach him – like the 'dropout' quoted in the last chapter – to doubt himself, he will 'leave school' even though his body remains for a few months more chained to a desk. If all we tell him, whether or not explicitly, is '*You* are a slow learner. *You* are a non-comprehender of teachers' questions', he will go on, slowly and uncomprehendingly, but increasingly convinced that real life is out of school, and he will *find himself* on the seat of a motor bike.

In some departments, however, where there is a fundamental concern with relationships and where objectives are often but not exclusively conceived in terms of social and emotional behaviour, contexts are created in which the pupil's language can be put to an extending range of uses. In such a climate his language itself may become the object of interested scrutiny, and thus some of the more exacting aims of the old academic curriculum may be attained even with those who, like the pupils of Abbey Wood, come from an area of uniform cultural and linguistic greyness. The importance of self-discovery needs emphasis on academic and linguistic grounds every bit as much as on considerations of adjustment and social behaviour. Every new situation in which the pupil is enabled to use language without excessive anxiety leads to a subtle modification or extension in his idea of himself. In so doing, *it opens him up for further learning*.

John Berger's remarkable book about a country doctor, *A Fortunate Man* contains a passage which not only summarizes most of my arguments so far, but forms an appropriate introduction to the work at Abbey Wood:

The inarticulateness of the English is the subject of many jokes and is often explained in terms of puritanism, shyness as a national characteristic, etc. This tends to obscure a more serious development. There are large sections of the English working and middle class who are inarticulate as the result of wholesale cultural deprivation. They are deprived of the means of translating what they know into thoughts which they can think. They have no examples to follow in which words clarify experience. Their spoken proverbial traditions have long been destroyed; and, although they are literate in the strictly technical sense, they have not had the opportunity of discovering the existence of a written cultural heritage.

Yet it is more than a question of literature. Any general culture acts as a mirror which enables the individual to recognize himself – or at least to recognize those parts of himself which are socially permissible. The culturally deprived have far fewer ways of recognizing themselves. A great deal of their experience – especially emotional and introspective experience – has to remain *unnamed* for them. Their chief means of self-expression is consequently through action; this is one of the reasons why the English have so many 'do-it-yourself' hobbies. The garden or the work bench becomes the nearest they have to a means of satisfactory introspection (Berger, 1968, p. 98).

It is a Friday afternoon. An unstreamed first-year class at Abbey Wood, like their young teacher, are within two hours of their first half-term holiday. The teacher has been trying to get them to decide on lines of work that might keep them going for some time; she offers further suggestions for some who seem slow to start – family, animals, football. On the blackboard she has already written:

1. Collection of stories	my family
2. Collection of poems	football
3. Stories, poems and facts	fishing
	animals
	the sea
	famous people
	fire

As I move round the desks I note some children copying poems from a well-known modern anthology. Two boys are working together on a large picture of a leopard; the thing is immensely vital, the boys quite absorbed. Several other children are drawing also. The teacher as she looks at their work reminds them that if they draw they must write something as well. Among topics on which individuals or pairs have apparently got started I note aeroplanes, football and animals; in each case the children have one or two reference books at hand. There is a loud buzz of conversation, not all about the work. Towards the end of the period the teacher wanders round with a notebook in which she records what each child is doing, and how far he has got.

The reader who was expecting this chapter to contain illustrations of enlightened modern practice – to contrast, perhaps, with situations cited in previous chapters – may wonder why I describe an inexperienced teacher in a rather fluid, inconclusive and even 'uninspiring' situation. I do so because it has a number of typical features and because its very untidiness may serve at the outset to remind us of the speciousness of tidy formulae for success. Here is a relative novice facing a teaching situation for which most of her own learning experience cannot have prepared her. Two features in particular are conducive to anxiety:

1. The wide range of ability among the children, which makes the group unlike most of those she herself was probably taught in.

2. The (relatively) free choice of activity open to the children. This of course follows partly from the ability-range within the class. Faced with a group so varied that while two or three might have entered a grammar school top stream, another four might have been placed in the remedial class of a secondary modern school – the responsible teacher cannot think in terms of mass-instruction.

In such circumstances my presence was hardly a help to her. At the end of the period she engagingly explained that she was 'new too' and confessed to have been 'floundering a bit' in her efforts to get the kids started on projects of their own choice. Her embarrassment and the thoughts that were going through her mind were obvious: 'He must think it's too noisy'; 'I don't expect it looks as if there's any work going on'. She would think I thought that precisely because a part of her, formed long ago, thought so too. 'After all, what progress *had* they made? Had they *learned* anything – had they learned *anything*?'

The answer to the last question must be a firm '*yes*'.* Their punctuation might be as bad as ever but they were learning different *hard* things. They were adjusting, firstly, to the attempt of the teacher to establish relationships with individuals, and a particular kind of atmosphere within the classroom. This might

* Cf. the testimony cited by Kohl, quoted on p. 105.

well have much in common with their experience in primary school, but it is unlikely to be characteristic of the *general* approach in the secondary school, even though things are improving. This means that they need time not only to adjust, but to reconcile *or merely accept* conflicting approaches and expectations within their new environment. This class had in fact made considerable adjustment – in only half a term – and learning had begun: learning to choose, to talk cooperatively, to sustain effort better, to call upon the teacher for help when needed.

Now it is very hard for a teacher to give children time in this way, very hard to accept that there is little to 'show for it all'. This is only true, however, if one is thinking exclusively in terms of essays written, grammar or dates learnt; there is a good deal to show if one looks for results in terms of social behaviour. The only way for the teacher to keep sane in these seemingly unproductive or chaotic waiting-times is to remind herself of the nature of her aims or rather, perhaps, to remind herself that she *has* aims. These have much to do with social behaviour in the classroom, with establishing the right climate of cooperative talk and sustained individual endeavour. Robertson and his colleagues saw the feasibility of subsequent learnings – including those of a more conventionally academic kind – as depending on an early education in *choosing*. In this, the teacher had three essential tasks to perform:

1. *Making things familiar*

In a sense the early days are a conducted tour, aimed at gently exploring the possibilities available, establishing a vocab. At the back of the teacher's mind may be a sort of linear progress through a range of activities which it is hoped the pupil will sample.

2. *Providing experience of success*

Although the range of activities may be extensive, care is taken to adjust the pace of the 'tour' – not every pupil sees or tries everything; some can be allowed to dawdle, to get fixated, until confidence grows. The aim is clearly to reach points in the tour early on where success may be achieved, and where a pupil may remain till he is ready to move on.

3. *Limiting the demands on the pupil's initiative*

Self-directed work comes only with the security of confidence; hence in the early stages the only options open to the pupil are planning options; these may be sufficient to suggest that he has some choice, but the choice is restricted enough not to be burdensome.

Another first-year mixed ability class were engaged, that Friday afternoon at Abbey Wood, on topics like 'The Story of My Life'. A good number, particularly of the girls, were working from family snapshots which they had brought into school and were pasting into exercise books to illustrate their accounts. Some of the photographs, inevitably, were diverting and so a good deal of the talk going on was family gossip. Such an activity is likely to be frowned upon by many teachers, whose attitude in this case seems doubly unfortunate. Just because a classroom presents a largely artificial situation, it does not follow that the exclusion of elements of 'real' life is a virtue; I have argued consistently that the less school life and 'real' life are interwoven, the less school means to the non-academic pupil. Not only this; to debar an activity such as that described is to miss a vital opportunity to *build upon* the purposes that language already serves for the child, for it ignores the extent to which gossip itself includes an element of the reflective thinking about human behaviour which is an essential part of work in the humanities. It may be true that the English teacher, by the nature of his subject, is more involved in the personal life of his pupils than are most of his colleagues, but the difference is one of degree. He would be as arrogant to suppose he had a monopoly in such matters as he would be stupid to see them as his sole concern. He will encourage pupils in their talking, writing and reading to confront questions like 'Who am I?' but this need imply no disregard for the technical competence that society continues to value, merely a belief that the latter is best founded on the former.

The discussion of failure by the four girls quoted in Appendix 1 (p. 175) shows something of the way 'mere gossip' develops into more deeply thoughtful, reflective talk. It is equally possible for certain kinds of absorbed personal writing to grow out of, and be sustained by, talk that explores feelings about people's behaviour. It is many years since Professor D. W. Harding first drew attention to the fact that gossip and literature were related ways of looking at and reflecting (enjoyably) upon experience. This idea is taken up and developed extensively by James Britton in *Language and Learning* (1970), where he illustrates the way our fascinated interest in others' behaviour finds expression in, for example, the post-mortems we like to hold after parties; as we tidy up after the last guest has departed, we ponder and speculate about how X looked, or why Z seemed unusually moody.

Where you have children comfortably listening to each other's voices and writings, the way is open for the introduction of literature. The relationship between the different aspects was brilliantly summed up by Douglas Barnes at the Dartmouth Seminar* :

It is through . . . talk that children can best find out in exchange with one another what are their responses to an experience, real or symbolic, and help one another to come to terms with it. Such talk does not occur in the classroom, however, without deliberate design; it is most likely when small groups of pupils talk about matters which engage their deepest attention. Nor will children talk in this way unless they feel that their responses and opinions are valued, and this has implications for the teacher's relationship with his pupils. *Works of literature enter this talk as voices contributing to the conversation, and the talk in its turn provides a context for literature,* which helps the children to take in what the voices have to say (quoted in Dixon, 1969, my italics).

The word 'literature' in the context above should not be taken in the old, somewhat exclusive sense. Participants at this Anglo-American Seminar agreed, remarkably, on a definition that embraced children's writing and film as well as books in general. In this sense it is obviously the concern of most teachers, its particular virtue being that it offers us a wider range of 'acquaintances' who help us, as we discuss them, to weigh the nature of our own experience and to grasp our own identity more firmly. It is because it fosters the growth of such awareness

*A very influential Anglo-American conference on English teaching held in 1966 at Dartmouth College, New Hampshire.

that early work in English at Abbey Wood was often based for several periods upon a novel (or a film) used as the core of a theme. An example of this, at fourth-year level, will be cited later in order to suggest the range of possibilities this approach opens up and the ways it offers support – as a clear-cut 'something-to-do' – to the inexperienced or insecure teacher. (For an extended and lively discussion of literature themes with young children the reader may like to consult Haggitt, 1967.)

While most of the class were talking over the story of their lives that afternoon, the snapshots enabling *even the weakest to write a few lines*, some children who for very good reasons would have fought shy of such a topic were working on quite different themes. Several were reading novels, and others were both writing and collecting poems. All seemed sufficiently engaged for the teacher to circulate and spend time with individuals who needed his help. I was particularly struck by the way this teacher tolerated the background buzz – he was content to wait in a way that assumed that out of the frivolous chat other kinds of exploratory, reflective or cooperative talk would grow. Two girls at a table near the front of the room were giggling rather a lot – apparently one of them had swallowed a tooth. After a while, as the teacher passed them, they told him their 'news'. He remarked briefly 'Oh, that's what you were talking about five minutes ago' and moved on to another table. This was not undiscriminating tolerance. Too early intervention by the teacher could have inhibited the development of the social security, the easy speech climate, that was his first aim. Later in the term he might perhaps judge the moment ripe to help the children to reflect, to focuss their experience.

'The Story of My Life' is an extended topic, likely to involve the pupils for a considerable time and consequently with varying degrees of absorption. Such work is clearly directed towards that rediscovery of the familiar* which is an important aspect of their learning to value, enjoy and profit from reflection about personal experience. Not only this, however; the extended framework used here permits the teacher to help them to learn to *sustain* their activity: he may indeed be less interested in a theme's subject matter, or the end-products to which some of

*For an extended discussion of this, see Creber (1968, ch. 2).

the work may lead, than in the pupils' acquisition of *certain habits of working*.

Conversely, where a teacher desires a briefer but more intense exploration of a personal theme he may employ what has been called the 'revisit strategy'. Here the content is in fact the same as might have been included in 'The Story of my Life' but by restricting the class to reflection about a single place – town, house or even room – that is vivid in their memory, the teacher hopes to prove to them just *how much* there is to say and write about experiences that otherwise might appear too banal to talk about. In all this work, moreover, we set up an expectation that the child has something to contribute, something we and his fellows will find interesting. By 'interesting', I don't mean unusual : the child's experience will interest us in the ways in which it differs from our own, but also and perhaps more importantly in the ways it resembles it. The writings of other pupils, like many novels and films, can offer support and reassurance to the adolescent, whose most persistent fear is that he is 'odd'. Richard Jones, in an important passage on the difference between the functions of the teacher and the therapist (1968, p. 78), emphasizes that the 'reduction of feelings of aloneness is the common denominator of all forms of psychotherapy', and goes on to suggest that the teacher's main concern is with 'outsight'* as opposed to insight. As he makes clear, however, the functions should be seen not as separate, but as having distinct emphases. In the context of the English work we have been considering, I think we can claim that the pupil is led to feel less alone in the course of activities which develop *both* insight and outsight.

By beginning with the assumption that the real expert about Billy's life is Billy himself, we shift the authority structure in the classroom, and by our acceptance and our valuing of his contribution, build up the confidence that must precede more fluent and more explicit 'self-exposure'. So a classroom atmosphere is established that depends above all upon mutual trust. We do not need, however, to think constantly in terms of self-

---

* 'Grasping, enlivening, enhancing, making one's own this-or-that datum in the real world – by virtue of gracing it with this-or-that private image.' (Jones, 1968).

exposure, of a too heavy concentration upon the personal, even private, life of the child. We can value him as an authority in other ways. Another teacher of first-year children I saw at Abbey Wood had been peculiarly successful in harnessing the distinctive hobbies or lines of interest of individual boys and girls.

The first two I noticed were in a private huddle, and one was reading to the other a story he'd written which, he announced proudly, he'd called 'The Fortune of War'. It was, in fact, rather good but what struck me most was the writer's gratification on discovering how much his listening partner liked it. Five minutes after the reading they were still talking it over. This incident in itself raises a host of issues, but two stand out as relevant to work in many subjects: the importance of listening; the effect upon a writer of having a 'real' audience (as opposed to the teacher) in promoting evaluative discussion. Another boy working on 'Birds' at that moment was doing a neat and scientific account of woodpeckers. A trio were working wittily and interestedly together on the same general topic. One, when questioned about his progress, said he was stuck — 'stuck for glue' and roared with laughter at his pun. A pair of girls in the corner were completely absorbed in the reading of a play, while just next to them two boys worked hard on a stage mock-up with paper figures. The amount of art material available and the efficient advice and suggestions of the teacher were alike impressive. Clearly her interest in art had been a powerful liberating influence. Yet it was not a dominating one, for in the far corner of the room sat a solitary lad, strikingly poor and unkempt in appearance, who for the whole forty minutes of the period lived in the world of the book in front of him. There was a good deal of noise in this room, but most of it was apparently related to the work in progress. When the bell went, signalling the beginning of the half-term holiday, 90 per cent of the class were quite obviously *working*.

Whether or not the teacher approaches the pupil's personal experience directly, a classroom climate like that illustrated above depends upon the generation of mutual trust. Probably nothing contributes to this so much as teacher's chat, the only stimulus which is infinitely adaptable. This does not mean egocentric ramblings about teacher's experience with the Eighth

Army – such ramblings insult the listener by *using* him for the speaker's own purposes – but the sort of chat where the teacher adds his own to the classroom pool of experience and invites others to do the same, building up confidence by constant soliciting of their views – Don't you think? What do *you* feel? etc.*
The current preoccupation with novel stimuli (to *goad* children into expression) and with mechanical aids has tended to obscure all this. When someone at the Walsall Seminar asked George Robertson. 'How do you introduce one of your themes?' it may have been in the expectation that he would reveal a sophisticated methodology, or audio-visual wizardry.

If this was the questioner's hope, he was disappointed.

'In the early stages, just through chat,' replied Robertson, and went on to outline a typical discussion on *disguises*. From a first, indirect, approach to the topic, encouraging talk about their dreams (both children's *and* teacher's), they might go on to look at some photographs and masks. Here the talk might lead to the discussion of faces that *are* masks. A further stage could be an introspective one, linked perhaps to the collecting of pictures, data, ideas. There would probably be discussion of films they had seen (e.g. an extract from a film called *Maggie,* a comedy about a businessman out of place – caught poaching). At this point they might be on the verge of critical thinking (Like it? What was it about? Gesture . . .? Use of camera . . .? etc.).

Condensed though it is, this example shows the pervasiveness of chat as well as suggesting further possibilities for work in a wide range of subjects. Such follow-up is only possible however when lessons are flexible and when the department is geared to the maximum availability of aids and materials. (*Hence the utter futility of the single 'English department' tape recorder, which is still the normal level of provision.*) Theme work demands that one kind of activity can lead to another without major disruption of the kind occasioned by children scouring the school for material that should be ready to hand. This kind of fluidity tends to frighten teachers only as long as they remain

*The relevance of Stenhouse's strictures about leading questions (see p. 128) appears to depend on the situation; here there is no emphasis on controversial material.

obsessed with the need to teach all the time. Watching a slightly hostile first-year class line up outside the room, a teacher was struck by the thought – 'What would happen if you all started to walk towards me?' So he shared the thought with them, and began their first work on drama with this classic exercise.

The important thing here is not simply that the teacher knew about dramatic possibilities but that he *watched* the children and, sensing something of their mood, turned it to advantage. To those used to a more conventional instructional role, I would stress that the crucial skill lies in the *sensing* rather than in the *exploitation* of the class mood. If one is open to experience, open to the children, attending to them, one is rarely at a loss for something to do, as the science teacher cited by Mackenzie (see p. 126) discovered. Something of this openness is evident in another example of theme work quoted by George Robertson at the Walsall Seminar.

Example of a first-year theme in action

English/Geography

Origin: Discussion between two heads of department of problems in language. They agreed that the children already had maps, *which they did not articulate,* of their neighbourhood, gangs, hideouts, etc.

Stage One: Talk.
Leading to maps of the area showing hideouts. During this they established the technical point that there are many maps of one place.

Stage Two: Demonstration.
Group of thirty kids took teacher around the estate, meeting people, collecting things that needed explaining and talking about: gypsies, man with a broken leg, unemployed man. This last led naturally to the question of what kinds of work were available and even to that common mystery – What precisely does Dad do?

In all this the geographers would stress, nowadays, the analysis of personal experience in order to acquire structure or concepts that the children can use on environments different from their own. From the English point of view, the most significant fact is that the pupils were assumed to have a great deal to contribute – this was a situation in which the teacher, literally, followed their lead.*

*The contrast with a 'closed' approach to environmental study of the kind typified by 'The 97 Bus' (p. 117) will be obvious.

I have stressed the first-year work at Abbey Wood because of the current tendency to 'add on' courses for adolescents, instead of making them the logical development of what has gone before. A great virtue of the work at Abbey Wood was the care with which the foundations were laid. Something of the way the English department sought to build upon them is suggested by the kind of working environment I found there among fourth-year classes.

The 'lesson' I saw George Robertson take with a fourth-year group began with a brisk 'stocktaking', the purpose of which was to ensure that those most in need received attention first. The tone, though friendly, was businesslike, and the pupils sorted themselves out and settled quite rapidly. It appeared that two boys were not in class that morning: one, who had lost all interest the previous year was out with a teacher who had a free period, driving around the estate; the other, who was virtually illiterate, had gone to the Man on the Moon Exhibition. Of those present:

three girls were reading *A Taste of Honey*
one girl was working from a collection of photographs
two boys were finishing a story called 'First Day Out'
two girls were working on the theme of 'Freedom' and
one boy was finishing a story on the same theme
three others were preparing a survey on attitudes to police to be used ultimately in an interview with some of the force
one boy was writing a letter to the school secretary asking for an interview
two were listening to a tape they had made of an interview with the headmistress
and two others were doing the same with a tape about three old people.

If we look more closely at some of these activities it will become easier to understand some of the processes that are the concern of the teacher. It is quite impossible, in any case, to describe this period as one would a 'lesson' of the old type since it has no meaning and no shape if considered in isolation from similar periods that had gone before. In particular I shall hope to show the extent to which the teacher is concerned with extending the child's *competence*, in a situation where literature is seen as a resource of absolutely central importance. I shall look at these two aspects in turn.

It is a commonplace of modern criticism to assert that the new emphasis on the creative aspect of English must be accompanied by a disregard for skills. It is true that we may begin by asking children to reflect upon their own experience and to express their feelings. Where such reflective and expressive work is effectively sustained, however, perception of oneself comes more and more to involve the consideration of language; language itself becomes an object of perception.* 'Free' work of the kind I saw at Abbey Wood is built upon a continuing process of consultation with the teacher. This process can become more searchingly evaluative as the child's freedom to initiate increases with experience. Consultation enables the teacher to diagnose something of the pupil's mood as well as the quality of his interest in the work on which he is engaged; it enables the teacher to sustain or revive impetus; and to offer a wide range of technical assistance, from advice on the choice of reading matter to help with the layout of a letter.

An example of this last occurred in the period I observed. The boy who wanted to interview the school secretary – and tape the encounter – had first to make a request. Early in the lesson he came to Robertson with his first draft and after discussion went away to re-write it. This is an obvious context for teacher advice but the range of technical discussion that arises from both taped interviews and questionnaires needs emphasis, particularly in view of the increasing use of these in work in the humanities. For example, the boys preparing the survey on attitudes to the police would have been involved in much more than the collection of material by talking to people. This would need to be noted down and the notes discussed to see whether they accurately conveyed the attitudes the boys had discovered. From this they would go on to consider what kind of questions to ask the police, and what statements to make about the attitudes they had encountered. This is meaningless unless it involves thought about tact, appropriateness in language. It may be that they

* For example the child's joke on p. 69 chapter two, or on p. 146 of this chapter.

would have to listen to tapes or broadcast interviews to clear up points of technique in the phrasing of interesting questions. This 'digression' might take a week of careful work, involving regular recourse to the teacher for advice.

The same kind of thing went on with the two groups who were listening to tapes. The pair working on 'Three Old People' decided, in consultation with the teacher, to add an introductory section to the tape beginning with:

1. Their own names, their class etc.
2. The title, 'Three Old People', clearly enunciated.
3. A brief explanation of the purpose of the tape.

Using rough paper and another tape they worked at 3 for the rest of the period before they were satisfied it was 'ready'. After seeing them purposefully engaged, Robertson listened to part of the interview with the headmistress which the other two boys had taped. When he went over to them they were already busy analysing what had gone wrong and working out new procedures. Their criticism of their own questions – which had been rather crude and uninspiring – was interesting but they became involved in deeper matters as they talked to their teacher. Much of their discussion with the headmistress had hinged on the kinds of freedom and privilege allowable to children of different ages. Since they had rapidly agreed that there had been 'too much headmistress and too little us' on the tape, the planning of new procedures was soon dealt with, and Robertson began to lead them to define their own attitudes more fully and more precisely. What did they mean by privilege? Was there no difference between the rights of first-year and sixth-formers? Where did fourth-formers come on the scale? And finally, after five minutes of this, he probed the differences between their point of view and that of the headmistress – was only one right? What was liberty, anyway? The response from a boy in the sixth or seventh stream showed that he had been led successfully to an uncharacteristic, and therefore all the more important, level of generalization: 'Well ... there's an adult way of looking at it ... and there's ours,' he said.

So much for the assumption that intellectual discussion is impossible with disadvantaged children. With the most disadvantaged of all, the problems are greater and the reader may assume that the near-illiterate who was away at the Man on the Moon Exhibition would be left in the vague hope that the experience would have 'done him good', somehow. Robertson's aim, however, was to enable him to articulate such experience. On his return the boy would follow an established routine: he would tape what he had to say, another boy would transcribe it, and Robertson would type it. After both transcription and typing the boy would read it, perhaps suggesting alterations. This technique is used quite widely here and in the USA with severely handicapped children and nearly always with good results. Its importance is emphasized by John Dixon:

To see and recognize one's own language on paper and as it's read aloud is a necessity for all children. Even John, the slowest of his class, was overjoyed when the words he dictated were read aloud by his teacher:

Fight with a Queen
Well see
   Suddenly I woke up, like
   I heard a terrible noise.
   I shot out of bed – like
   I put on some clothes
   And snatched a sword
   From the wall.
   I shot out of the room, like
   Waving the sword up and down
   I rushed into the hall, like
And see
   I saw goblins
   trying to catch the guards, like
   I stamped on the goblins feet
   Suddenly I saw Goblin Queen,
   She hit me and lifted me up, like
   I swiped the sword
   On the side of her face, like.

(J. Dixon, citing Mrs Buttrey's evidence, in Briefing Paper to Walsall Seminar)

As Dixon goes on to point out, as soon as something is written down it becomes different from what might have been said, and this difference increasingly becomes a subject of interest to children.

I have so far stressed the teacher's consultative role in this fluid 'workshop' situation as a means whereby competence is developed. Perhaps even more important – creating the basic situation in which his help is *felt* to be needed – is the cooperative talk which accompanies most activities of the project or workshop type. In the examples I have cited already it must be clear that the teacher does not initiate evaluation or analysis: nearly always he builds on something that is already there – Robertson did not need to *tell* the two boys that their tape recorded too little of their own talk. In examples quoted of first-year work the same elements of self-critical appraisal appear clearly in almost every genuinely cooperative and absorbing enterprise: the two boys mentioned who were building a model stage set, for instance, were continually consulting each other, and even when most absorbed each would occasionally look up to see how his partner was getting on.

More striking perhaps was the instance of the boy reading to his friend his story 'The Fortunes of War' and being delighted that his friend enjoyed it. The importance of children sharing their work in this way can hardly be overemphasized; the praise and criticism of peers come easily, generally do not wound, and stimulate renewed effort. Improvement in language depends upon the development of standards that are meaningful and an audience of peers is frequently a more important spur in this than any reactions of the teacher. Given such an audience, the child normally wants to improve and his writing soon becomes coloured by his growing sense of the audience he is writing for. In time this sense becomes part of his critical apparatus until, for most purposes, the self is audience enough. The teacher's task is to set up frameworks in which this process of development can take place, rather than to impose standards. He may be confident that as improvements, or presentation, or even hand-writing begin to *matter* to the child he will seek help or advice.

If one accepts that improvement in language-use is an aim appropriate to a much wider sector of the curriculum than the five or six periods which the timetable designates 'English', the progress towards self-evaluation of the kind described may be seen to have equally wide relevance. In most subjects little attention has been paid to it, however. This is certainly true in English, where the recent emphasis has been upon 'creative' expression while follow-up processes of evaluation and improvement have been neglected. This is partly the result of uncertainty; the desire to avoid the old errors of that teacher's role which Andrew Wilkinson satirized as 'the teacher as printer's reader' – a lynx-eyed error-detector – this desire has been praiseworthy but it has left a vacuum – how do I mark it if not out of ten? The answer seems clear – hand part of the responsibility for evaluation over to the pupil, or to the group. The process begins when we encourage them simply to look at each other's work.

This is by no means as pie-eyed as it may seem. In general the idea of workshop – as a fluid and flexible teaching environment, one activity leading naturally to another – has gained ground since the Anglo-American Seminar at Dartmouth. A corollary of this idea must be that the workshop is a place where the *crafts* of language are played with, enjoyed, experimented with and, later, *analysed*. Such self-analysis is a natural part of the work of a 'creative' author; it is also something towards which we need to work in our encouragement of self-expression. Robertson cited the case of a child in the second year who spent *as much time* reading and re-working her poems as in writing them. Once the basic situation – cooperative discussion leading to revision – has been set up, the teacher will find ample opportunity to introduce all the *teaching* he could wish for. More than this, he will probably discover that technical concepts can challenge the child and renew rather than dampen motivation.

The discussion of literature may be seen as merely a logical extension of the talking-over of each other's experiences, expressed in speech and writing, that has been going on since the first year. Often it will enable the class to grapple with more explicit treatments of topics upon which a pupil's own reflections – if at all genuine – can hardly be made the subject of general discussion. As Sidney Bolt pointed out (see p. 61), literature is particular enough to promote the involvement that is required if insight and understanding are to be deepened. It can also afford the special kind of reassurance that the adolescent – beset by the quite normal conviction of his own oddity – particularly needs: it deals with situations close enough to his own for him to discover more about himself, yet sufficiently distinct for him to make such discoveries without undue embarrassment. Almost inevitably such discoveries prompt further self-exploration in both talk and writing.

As the quotation from Barnes suggested (see p. 143), however, this happens only when works of literature enter group or class discussion 'as voices contributing to the conversation' and the 'talk in turn provides a context for literature'. This demands of the teacher a two-fold expertise. He has to set up the situation into which a literary voice can enter *without interrupting or drowning* the rest of the conversation. And, secondly, he has to have the requisite literary resources. There can hardly be a more searching criterion of quality in an English teacher than his capacity to use literature 'contextually'. Beside the demands that this makes upon his literary knowledge, his resources and his insight into children, the teaching of set texts to the upper sixth is straightforward. This may seem depressing but the difficulties are considerably reduced – and the teacher's own literary resource and knowledge extended – if he works in a department where the pooling of books, films and extracts, as well as ideas, is customary procedure.

In the fourth-year lesson I saw, the three girls reading *A Taste of Honey* had been led to it through apparently casual chat. The boys and girls working on topics like 'Freedom' or 'First Day Out' had been read the date analysis of the man's early life in *The Unknown Citizen*. This had whetted their appetite and led to the demand by the class for more, in particular the chapter where the man comes out of prison. The fact that the teacher works largely with small groups much of whose work by now is self-initiated need not mean that there is no longer a place for the class as a whole to be read some part of a book. Robertson finds such readings useful starting points for a variety of activities but believes that they also provide necessary opportunities for the class to come together to share experiences. These have a cohesive effect upon the group and act as reference points in the term or year to which the teacher can often usefully appeal. This may be made clear by the following example which he submitted to the Walsall Seminar.

Example of a fourth- to fifth-year theme

GENERAL AIM: to set up the kinds of classroom activity/situation that enables students to approach each other as adults, without any shock of confrontation, or the need for it.

METHOD: introduction into informal class situation of a powerful bit of literature.

TEACHER READS: Tom and Becky proposal scene from *Tom Sawyer*.

REACTION: Kids laugh.

QUESTION: But are Tom and Becky just little kids?

HE: Reads from *Under Milkwood*, Mr and Mrs Pugh.

QUESTION: How do you get from the first to the second extract?

At this point the library, together with the filing cabinet of extracts, references of all kinds filed under topic headings, is thrown open to the students to explore, after which the teacher reads more material:

The finding of the baby from *The Caucasian Chalk Circle*.
Poems on similar theme, e.g. MacNeice's *Prayer before Birth*.

I have sought to emphasize that the kind of classroom organization found at Abbey Wood (uncommon, but happily not unique) actually facilitates a number of activities that in their *rigour* and *technicality* are of kind not normally associated with such teaching situations. The same is true of literary study that can go on. The example quoted above, particularly, of course, the reference to Brecht, provoked from the listening group at Walsall the assertion that we could no longer be talking about deprived kids. To this Robertson responded by proclaiming his 'passionate conviction' that 'there is no child/adult without the potentiality to respond to high literature'. The thing was to engineer situations and stories that took the kids just that bit further than they knew they could go, often but not always using contemporary literature.

This seems to me an optimistic but, because of that, a fruitful approach. We have been far too ready to base our planning for the deprived on the mere avoidance of what we 'knew' they couldn't do. This is not only bad for the kids, it is bad for the teacher also. The section of his book in which Tom Haggitt describes how he used *Of Mice and Men* with ten year olds* illustrates the surprising discoveries about children's capacities that can follow an optimistic initiative by the teacher. Robertson's approach reveals a similar optimism but is less teacher-directed. It shows how an education in choosing can lead to progressively wider freedoms in which more and more of the child's learning is self-initiated. This is particularly important at a time when we are only just beginning to realize the possibilities that attend the systematic development of child-initiative.

I have described some of the work at two age levels in a remarkable English Department. The purpose of this is not to hold up some impossible ideal; it is in fact easy to move *in this direction* and the basic approaches are relevant to current development work *in much of the curriculum*. To move far, however, there must be a continual, professional, pooling of ideas† and proper systems for ensuring that good teaching material is collected in some kind of central filing system (the work is exhausting but we can at least lighten the burden by preventing wastage of ideas). It seems only appropriate to conclude this section by letting the architect speak for himself:

Literature and creative writing are important as concentrated and specialized developments of processes which reach into a vast range of activities. (Thus, I do not, for instance, necessarily take a particular poem and work it with the whole class. I may give it to a group in the class because their level of discussion seems right to deal usefully with it; to another pupil because it echoes some aspect of his experience; to another to extend a sociological inquiry on an imaginative level. And so on.) But talk, of all sorts, rightly set in context, has just as enormous importance – there must be talk. So also there must be the chance to act out, explore all sorts of social and working situations, and to meet all sorts of experiences other than verbal ones, because these all have unique power to call forth kinds of language.

If I may have pupils in one classroom simultaneously engaged in reading Carlyle on the French Revolution
using a programmed punctuation book
discussing their last piece of writing

*Tom Haggitt (1967), having seen this work in progress I can testify to the modesty of his account.
†This includes seeing them in action.

analysing a case history of R. D. Laing's book on schizophrenia
reading poems aloud
taping a discussion on race
painting
talking about their row with the boyfriend
many writing poems and stories
many just reading
studying a film strip, etc., etc.

this does not represent the last stages of permissive collapse; it is the product of implicity and explicitly inviting the pupils to engage, with the teacher, in a two-fold inquiry of a particular nature. It is an inquiry into meanings in which we are simultaneously trying to articulate what x is and means, and what it means to 'me'. It is also an inquiry into what mode of language best serves this inquiry in which it is the teacher's responsibility to see that the situation, the materials and the models of language and thought which are offered, suit both the intrinsic values of the subject matter and the capacities and capabilities of the student.

In a room and indeed a school, in which resources in all media are available, and visits out encouraged, I value the interaction of pupils of different abilities and ages. The planning of the geography of the classroom and the stacking and supply of resources become crucial.

Here, the pupil engages with his environment. The teacher, who has created the environment, then enters into that engagement in whatever role serves best (Robertson, 1969).

5 Teacher Training and the Way Ahead

At the Walsall Seminar a briefing paper on 'Technological teaching' by Ronald Higday, a teacher from California, conjured up this vision of the future:

Students needing help with standard English usage drill themselves with materials pre-programmed on a dual track audio response tape recorder or practise following the instructor's model on Language Master cards.... Similar material programmed on audio response equipment is the main source of drill material for students learning standard English as a second dialect. The same students use a television camera and video recorder to see and hear themselves practising their new dialect.... The same video recording equipment provides students of formal speech techniques with a far more meaningful evaluation than that provided by a teacher's criticism.... A composition student progresses at his own speed through a programmed set of transparencies on the overhead projector, turning to the teacher only for evaluation or progress reports.... A student who has reading difficulties listens over a headset to a dramatically read, verbatim tape recording of a novel, while following the reading in his text.... A very capable reader listens to portions of a similar dramatic recording of literature to get an interpretation of tone, mood or character. ... A student interested in the history of language studies the development of language families with the help of programmed materials on a teaching machine.... A group of students whose interest is juvenile delinquency use a rear screen projector and individual headsets to watch a movie, *The Blackboard Jungle*.... A group of students use sounds gathered in the community with a portable tape recorder to enhance the dramatization of a short story.... Two students working behind a screen, immerse themselves in a psychedelic light show as the basis for a creative writing project.... A group of students use the video recorder to watch a documentary film pretaped by the instructor.

That may all seem as remote as the most advanced space fiction, yet it is in fact only an extension of the way Higday in an experimental school in a deprived area is able to work *now*, for part of the time. Certainly it may serve to underline the paucity of 'hardware' – the whole range of aids available in our own schools. We need more, and it needs to be better used.* Higday was concerned to present it as a means of setting up individualized teaching; the aids were merely machines whose function was to free the teacher from various chores and to 'amplify the force of his creative and distinctively human efforts'.

By itself, the provision of mechanical aids can have only a marginal impact on the problems I have outlined. The real answer has been implicit throughout – more teachers, better equipped and 'equipped' here implies more than the provision of the necessary hardware. It implies adequate training both before and after the teacher gains his initial teaching qualification. Even the training is not enough; above all, the teacher needs a feasible working environment in which, ideally, the working out of a concerted language policy is accepted as an indispensable part of professional responsibility.

Part of a letter from one of the best students I have had, now in his sixth year of teaching, may serve to suggest the gap between the ideal and the actual situation. Alan's remarks remind us how hard we make it even for good teachers and relatively able pupils and suggest that the amount of theoretical discussion now going on about the curriculum may be a misleading indication of conditions in the average school. It also provides a further refutation of the notion that educational deprivation is the lot of any particular social or intellectual minority:

I have no room of my own; the English department tape recorder is in the grasping hands of the geography department, there is no television and no radio and no acquiescence in the plea of the second-in-department and myself for getting hold of those wonderful BBC pamphlets; I have no cupboard in a classroom for essential teaching books, which consequently are often stolen; every day a boy loses or has stolen a textbook or exercise book and nobody seems prepared to tackle the problem. The English stock room is used for Latin and

*Even traditional aids are distributed with myopic parsimony. A recent survey by the Publishers Association and the Association of Education Committees has revealed scandalous underspending by many authorities. Moreover their evidence suggests that the situation is getting worse (see *The Times Educational Supplement*, 5 March 1971).

R.I. teaching and looks like a burgled bedroom and the overflow of stock into the Library Annexe is tossed around by most of the boys who are taught there (usually thirty of them crammed into a room fit for fifteen); and the Head of Department refuses to coordinate or consult his men or take any interest in the type of teaching we are doing. This, I assure you, is an objective catalogue, written rapidly – I dare not try to think too hard. Are *all* second-rate grammar schools like this? Because I had not a quarter of these complaints at down-on-its-beam-ends – County Secondary!

Miraculously – because of a 'wonderful inside-the-classroom freedom', the obverse of the isolation criticized in chapter three – Alan still enjoys teaching, but it remains evident that no basic, first course of professional training can prepare a teacher to survive indefinitely on his own resources. The schools must provide a working environment where the professional interchange of ideas is a normal part of the teacher's life. Where such working conditions obtain, the school itself largely fulfils the need for continued ('in-service') training; the children also benefit, being well taught when teachers are still regularly learning from each other. These schools cannot of course meet the whole demand for in-service training but they offer significant guide-lines: they suggest above all the need for such training to be linked to *operations* – to workshop situations as opposed to traditional courses of lectures. The fact is that the *behaviour* of few teachers (and few children) is directly modified by listening unless it is part of a doing situation. The old lecture courses for teachers have reassured the converted, appeased the fears of the anxious (momentarily), furthered the career designs of the ambitious and the overweening; in a depressingly small proportion of cases have they significantly affected subsequent teaching. This is largely because they have carried intellectual authority rather than emotional conviction. There is little chance of altering or improving the performance of the practising teacher unless we convince him that *he can do it*. The schools that foster a continual exchange of ideas among the staff also breed the confidence the teacher needs before he can change or experiment.

In this connection the setting up of the new teachers' centres marks a significant advance. The equipment and the payment of the wardens of these centres is often inadequate but the foundation has been laid for the systematic encouragement of professional discussion; inadequate funds have been a blessing too in some areas, for the emphasis from the start has had to be on *self-help*. In order to accelerate progress, however, further incentives are needed. Too few centres at present are well supported by staff in *both* primary and secondary schools; some have had particular difficulty in engaging the interest of secondary teachers. Here we see the effects of the old 'self-sufficiency' theory, not to mention the fact that until recently the training of graduates has been regarded as an optional extra.

The difficulty of establishing the idea that a teacher's training, far from being a once-and-for-all affair, is a continuing process; that periodic 'refreshment' or retraining is a professional obligation, is not merely the result of past inadequacies in in-service training. To a considerable extent it arises from deficiencies in those courses by which students gained their initial qualifications to teach. These bred a scepticism towards training that was tacitly reinforced by a system which allowed untrained graduates to become recognized as teachers after a brief probationary (sic) period. Nor did the experience of many graduates who sacrificed a year's gainful employment in order to train suggest that their less conscientious colleagues were mistaken. There can be no doubt that students have had legitimate grounds for complaint, particularly over the number of teacher trainers in both college and university who, though academically well qualified, are inexperienced or demonstrably incompetent in classroom situations.

There have been improvements in recent years, not least because students have become more outspoken in their criticisms and have in consequence been heard, occasionally.* At the time of writing teacher training is under review but the manner of its inception and the ludicrous speed with which various unwieldly, but highly representative, groups are expected to draw and pass on conclusions from masses of intractable material offer little grounds for optimism.

We have a long way to go before school and training establishments work together in the sort of partnership that is needed.

* See, for example, Evidence of the National Union of Students on Teacher Training to the Plowden Committee, HMSO.

The student's most legitimate complaint arises from the painful and disconcerting discovery that the school where he is 'practising' speaks with a voice quite different from that he has been used to in College or University. Not only this; too many schools, though ready to plead for more or better teachers, continue evidently to resent students as a nuisance. That they may be so – particularly in large urban areas where the number of training establishments means that schools have to endure a major invasion each term – is undeniable. But the same resentment is sometimes found in schools which suffer no such burden. The diffused effect of such resentment – however justified – is to undermine students' confidence in what they are doing. In the following poem, a student reflects upon his experience in teaching practice, brilliantly evoking a common predicament.

2W
Outside the grass was being cut by a motor-mower cowboy
And I was reading 'An Irish Airman forsees his Death'
To thirty striped blazers, one or two faces and a Tutor.
I was a salesman he had said. 'You've got your brushes –
You have got to sell them.' (He should have mentioned polish
To be metaphorically complete; if not funny).
So there I was; the new student broom, sweeping
Clouds of Yeats into my face.

4H
They are quiet now because they do not want to miss
A 'Dirty Word', like thigh, or breast, erection, even 'piss'.
They are adolescent seals waiting for me to throw the fishy words
That make them choke and splutter, giggling for more.
Even the ginger one has closed *The Ginger Man* he reads
Beneath the desk. Appropriately enough.
Their eyes are full of my unuttered four letter words.
The 'Liverpool Scene' and not heard.

4T
I continue to read contemporary poetry
To my temporary audience.
All thirty-three sitting behind drawing boards.
Poetry will be in the Technical Drawing Office,
Where four keen, sixth-formers sit at the back.
Their backs to me,
Drawing, technically.
I read *The Execution of Cornelius Vane* by Herbert Read.

There is no laughter at the word 'piss'.
Half-way through I notice the four, keen, sixth-formers
Have stopped. Drawing. Technically.
They are listening. I am winning.
I go back to the staff room.
I am required to stop. Reading. Dirty Poems.
'He saw a party of his own regiment,
With rifles, looking very sad.
The morning was bright, and as they tied
The cloth over his eyes, he said to the assembly:
"What wrong have I done that I should leave these..."'
Before I left I was told.
You must give them more written work –
To copy – AND LESS ENTERTAINMENT,
'I say, I say, I say. A funny thing
Happened to me on the way to the class
A very ugly yob came up to me –
(Little did he know that I knew
That his mother had left home
That every night he went home to nothing
Until his elder brother came in.
Usually beating him)
And said – (wait for it kids)
"Sir, can we have some more poetry?"
Laugh! –
Well I hope you enjoyed the show
And now the Massed Bans
Of your own LEA'

The headmaster said I had been too lenient
(If they are glad to see you go, then you have succeeded.)
'You have to be a real bastard at first', he said.
I nodded, obsessed by his twisted smile,
Remembering that canes are listed in catalogues
Under 'Teaching Aids'.
The metalwork master said: –
'That little bugger in 4H, Williams –
Swearing in my lesson. I caned the bastard.'
I practised my twisted smile.
Remembering that canes should be listed
In catalogues under 'Bloody sodding Teaching Bloody Aids'.

I left the school on a windy Friday.
I left the school during a staff meeting

I left twenty-three adults discussing,
As they had discussed for twenty minutes
Whether to ring the morning bell
At 9.5 or 9.10. Or was it
  9.7 or 9.12
Or 9.3 or 9.7 a.m.
I affirm that I am not consciously
Looking for Symbols.

P.R. (reproduced by permission of the editor of *Accent,* St. Luke's
College, Exeter)

Here we see the student's most typical dilemma: to arouse the
pupils' interest is one thing; at the same time to avoid offending
against assumptions and principles that underlie the school's
organization is quite another.*

As a teacher trainer who frequently sees students coping with
this problem I sympathize with this student in his encounter
with what seem to him authoritarian or obsessive attitudes.
The dichotomy, persistently invoked by the cynical old hands in
the staff room, between life at the coal-face (practice – what is
feasible in schools) and at the pit-head (theory – what is
preached in colleges of education etc.) is, however, as much the
product of inadequate teacher preparation as of shortcomings
among the practitioners. It is partly true that teachers are prepared for 'ideal' situations and that those who survive the decep-
tion emerge with philosophies learnt in the *sauve-qui-peut*
school. As a result, 'theory' becomes a dirty word.

It is unfortunate that the 'practical' is more acceptable in our
culture than the 'theoretical', for what is often needed in the
teaching situation is a reinstatement of 'theory'; even the most
practical man – who canes every little Williams he can lay hands
on – operates from an unrealized and unarticulated theoretical
framework. We need to face very squarely with students the
issues raised by the inevitable confrontation with the stock
response, 'That may be very well in *theory* but in practice ...'
In fact, if it's not right in educational practice, it's bad educational theory.

At the Walsall Seminar a study group on teacher training

*Hannam, Smyth and Stephenson (1971) provides an absorbing com-
mentary on this and other issues with which this chapter is concerned.

began its report by emphasizing the reciprocal relationship between the teacher-training institution and the school and asked two questions:

What help can the colleges give the schools with their disadvantaged children?
What help can the schools give in the effective training of teachers?

These questions served to focus attention on two main areas of need:

Of disadvantaged children for more contact with friendly adults – there just weren't enough in the schools to 'go round'.
Of students in training for the opportunity to learn to enjoy working with children, to become attuned to their responses, their talk and their feelings.

The solutions of these needs the study group saw as interdependent:

If the colleges are determined to make a contribution to the education of the disadvantaged child, they need to extend and coordinate the links with school teachers and children. We believe that a training course for teachers should provide opportunities to meet a variety of the student teachers' needs, e.g.:

1. Need to respond to individual children.

2. Need to help children to work in small groups.

3. Need to study within these groups linguistically deprived children and help them to overcome these difficulties.

4. Need for an understanding of group and individual psychology.

5. Need to understand themselves in this situation.

6. Need to learn about and understand the local community and its effects on children, to understand individual children within that community.

7. Need to understand the processes of thought.

8. Need to understand how a child's linguistic skill develops.

All these opportunities are available in the schools, but as teaching practice is organized in the majority of our schools and colleges, these opportunities are not being used to the best advantage of students and children.

While teacher trainers have been prepared to advocate child-centred methods of teaching, there has been some reluctance to apply the same principle within their own institutions. It is certainly hard to see how one could meet the students' needs as listed above without in fact devising a student-centred training course. Three aspects of such a course – theoretical, practical and expressive – are worth considering further.

Student-centred training
Theoretical aspects

Under this heading come the parts of the college syllabus that are at present normally split between 'main subject' and 'Education'. The latter may be subdivided into psychology of education, sociology, history, philosophy, etc., while the former, for an intending English teacher, for example, will be mostly about literature. This framework has been adopted as:

1. Economic – permitting, for example, the psychologist to run a basic course on psychology for several groups of students.
2. Intellectually respectable – the fear is constantly that the content may be watered down, that the psychology may become mere common sense or that the English course may not be literary enough.

In other words the 'disciplines' must be kept pure. I do not want to develop the familiar criticism that all this leads in practice to psychology which has more to do with rats in mazes than with students and the children they teach, and to English which provides a scaled-down version of an inclusive university syllabus – a Cook's tour of literature. There is some truth in the argument, but I would rather attack the 'purists' more fundamentally for their mistaken assumption that rigorous thinking can only go on within a framework of the traditional compartments of learning. This is controverted every day by one's own observation of the way students learn best. Not only this, the exponents of pure academic disciplines within teacher training are largely responsible for the widespread undervaluation of all that is now implied by remedial work. How otherwise can one account for the popular notion that such work demands sympathy, patience, good temperament, sense of vocation but that, somehow, intellectual qualities – above the level of practical horse-sense – are superfluous? I cannot see the way to reinvest teacher training with *intellectual* rigour *except* through frameworks based on an appreciation of student needs. In practice this would mean that:

1. Elementary psychological/sociological concepts would be communicated by main-subject tutors largely in the context of, or as a follow-up to, the in-school experience of groups of students.
2. The psychologists, sociologists, etc. would increasingly be regarded as resource persons to guide and comment on work carried out in schools with real children. It may be recalled that the fifth need in the list related to the students' understanding of *themselves* as they confront disadvantaged children and here again the psychologists and sociologists have a contribution to make, helping students to understand the ways in which they have been conditioned.

The Walsall Study Group on teacher training recognized the vulnerability of students in down-town schools where a high proportion of the pupils have personal, social and learning problems. They saw little merit, however, in merely delaying the students' exposure to such situations, for the number of disadvantaged children was growing and many of the best young teachers in fact wanted to teach in areas where they were particularly needed. The most hopeful solution, providing both the necessary moral support and a context for theoretical learning, lay in situations where groups of students worked together in schools:

We envisage a pattern of cooperative work in which tutors and students from the colleges and teachers from the schools are engaged. The work in the schools in which the students are to share will have been fully discussed and shaped by tutors and teachers in advance. Students will have been prepared for the work by their tutors and will be incorporated into the work in the school. The tutor and his group of students will work with the school ideally for a year. Students could work, for example, first with small groups, then with the class teacher and then perhaps with a team. In the schools there will be follow-up discussions about the work in progress and the development of the children, discussions in which tutor, students and teachers will take part. Back at the college, the experiences met in schools will be studied in depth and given the appropriate philosophical, psychological or sociological perspective. In this way, theory and practice should feed and supplement each other and teaching practice would fill its proper role in the students' development.

In all this there is assumed the need for a new kind of partnership between school and training establishment. Such an approach is seen not only as a means of improving teacher training, however, but as a way in which groups of interested (and partly informed) adults may be brought in to supply additional manpower where it is most needed.*

Practical aspects

What has to be said here has already been partly implied in the suggestion that the theoretical work needs to be related as far as possible to situations in which students meet children. The first point to be made is simply that the students need to *make contact*. The idea that they are there to teach may initially be a distraction, if not an irrelevance. Connie Rosen's paper on teacher training for the Walsall Seminar gives a picture of the kind of situations in which contact can be made.

In these meetings with the small groups of children, the students have taken them to look at the cement mixer, the pet shop and the park. They have taken in things for the children to look at and talk about, have read them poems and stories, have worked on number apparatus, and drawn and painted. They have talked with them about their families, their pets, their interests and have mounted the children's work in books so that the children can take pleasure in the final results. We spend some tutorial time talking about the children and what they're doing together. We have looked at suitable poems and story books. We have examined readers. We have discussed the kind of help the children need to get their thoughts on to paper. We look as though we're all travelling along together very amicably with the idea that they provide the experience, the talk, the materials and the help. It's all very enjoyable and the children look forward to their visits. But the students are cautious. This can't be English, this cem-

*This approach is already being tried out in 'educational priority areas' of Liverpool and the first indications from the use of students in this way are thoroughly encouraging.

ent mixer and chrysanthemums and autumn leaves, this talking and painting and drawing and making. There is still a long, long road ahead.

As the last sentence implies, the students will show varying degrees of resistance or anxiety in this situation. Some of this quite simply will have to be tolerated, but not all: the fear that they are not getting on with the job is largely allayed where their experience and observations are properly related to theoretical work in child development, on language and thought especially. In this way one is working towards aims similar to those which underlay the old stipulation in colleges that all students, no matter what their specialist subject, should do some 'basic' English teaching.

In so far as this recognized the importance of language it was, I suppose, praiseworthy. Its practical consequences were frequently unfortunate, however; on the one hand the student specializing in maths or craft saw his weekly two periods of English as a chore because their underlying purpose was never clear to him, was not part of an overall emphasis on the place of language in learning; on the other hand, the children were subjected to a great number of lessons that ranged from the boring to the totally incompetent. The assumptions underlying this stipulation were in fact mistaken – why, if language is so important, should it be studied only in relation to work in English? What the student requires is not two periods of English as an irrelevant extra, but guidance and theoretical instruction about the role of language in learning, particularly learning in *his* subject. And it makes no difference whether his subject is religious education or metalwork. Such a new emphasis needs to become a standard element of teaching practice if we are to refashion ideas about language in a way that accords with what we now know about it. To approach it in this way, as an aspect of every specialist subject, is to invest it with real interest for those who would find basic English a total irrelevance. This is not all: to attend to language in metalwork leads to better language, but also to better metalwork. As John Dixon puts it:

using language to operate on experience is characteristic of most academic subjects (at their best), and this involves learning to use language in new ways, and with new variety, as pupils encounter the earlier stages of each subject discipline. Thus even so-called 'practical' subjects, like the crafts, may incorporate a good deal of planning and thinking over, some of it verbalized, some visual (in diagrams and sketches): anyone who has watched a group of boys designing and making something like a go-kart would acknowledge the complexity and value of the relationship between language and 'practical' activity. In scientific disciplines, too, the preliminary observations, the exact framing of hypotheses (and the choice between them), and the elaboration of verifying experiments, all involve language. Such language operates at several levels of abstraction, from the simplest one of playing a role in the selection of relevant material from the mass of all that is observed, to the complex levels that permit a critical awareness of the conceptual framework to which the hypothesis relates. . . .

If pupils are to take from a subject what it has to offer, all specialists must realize the roles that language plays. Traditionally, language has been viewed as a 'vehicle' for knowledge, a conception encouraged by the appearance in notebooks and examination papers of words that echoed those printed in the textbook. . . . The significance of talk has been too often ignored, though it is increasingly used in the new developments of school maths, science, etc. A personal response has been felt to be rather irrelevant: why trouble about 'what is going on inside pupils when they are given a frog to dissect or stop to admire the bright blue inside a test tube or are moved by a moment of history'? (Dixon, 1969, pp. 67–8).

Expressive aspects

The theoretical and practical aspects already discussed are incomplete without provision for the students' own expressive activity. This is best seen as complementary to the theoretical learning, for it also helps the student to understand himself, and the children through his own childhood. We have seen the anxieties that novel classroom situations engender, and the intellectual and emotional demands they make of the teacher. In these circumstances we need to pay attention to all activities talk, art, craft, drama, music, dance – which may increase confidence and induce the emotional balance and security which are needed. As we saw in chapter two, the teacher as well as the child needs to be 'psychologically safe'. In a three- or four-year course we have a great opportunity to pay proper attention to the teachers' own emotional development but if we fail – so that when he comes into the classroom he still feels bound to leave half his personality outside – then the outlook is grim. Indeed, the prospect of generations of future students inhibitedly utilizing techniques designed to deinhibit their pupils is too horrible to contemplate.

Opposing intellectual to emotional development is to make a virtue of a contingent happening, not a necessity; it is to encourage a schizoid split in the personality of modern intellectual and technological man which tends to make him impotent in attempting to reconcile his ideals with his actual behaviour. Emotion is not something to be refined on its own but the energizing element in all creative thought. Hence to make an opposition between the academic and the pastoral aims of a college of education is to exacerbate the already difficult task of energizing intellectual effort. I agree with Bantock that by and large college students do not exhibit the intellectual robustness we would both like to see, but the failure here is a failure to see that student well-being has to be both intellectual and emotional. Where the attempt is made to make it one or the other, the door is wide open to the production of either the conformist individual or the ineffective rebel or dropout.

To depict the relation between teacher and pupil as one which requires either that the teacher and his subject or that the pupil or student should be the focus of endeavour, is to ignore the plain fact that what we are dealing with is a case of interaction, and that what is crucial is the model of interaction which we approve. The interaction may take the form of education in which the teacher manipulates the pupil or student i.e. causes things to be done *to* him, or it may take the form of learning by the pupil, in which much is done *for* him, or it may take the form of a genuine partnership, a doing together, in which teacher and pupil learn from one another, although at different levels (Morris, 1969, pp. 137–8).

At the end of the Walsall Seminar a statement was issued to the press. This particularly stressed the children's need for 'a stable relationship with a skilled and trusted adult'. Such a need could not be met as long as we tolerated a situation in which, for example, the head teacher of an urban infants' school had to work with a group of one hundred and thirty for a term, in which brief span of time children in another primary school class had twenty teachers. Conditions such as these meant that secondary schools could only attempt 'to contain failure' but they could be ameliorated by the redeployment of human resources in training establishments. The statement concluded with a *Summary of Aims*:

1. We must seek to enable the full personal growth of the many children who now leave school undeveloped or maimed in personality.

2. We seek to give them a greater awareness of their identity in the community; a greater awareness of that community, and of its needs and resources; and a greater mastery of the language skills that it demands of us.

3. We seek to organize schools in such a way that everything about them enables this personal and social development to take place through the richness of the school environment and the skills of the teachers.

4. We need the kind of teachers who can do this work; we need conditions in which they can do it: and we must enable them to develop in their work.

These are themes with which I have been concerned throughout this book. More especially I have sought to show the way in which we place not merely a minority but perhaps a majority of children at a disadvantage through the kinds of language environment we provide for them.

Billy Casper, hero of the film *Kes* (1970)* is the archetype of the disadvantaged child. Apparently non-verbal, though capable of extra-curricular wit and resource, he dreams his way through a school world which only rarely impinges on his own interior life. Fatherless, occasionally indulged but never understood by a mother preoccupied with her own need for understanding and satisfaction, terrified of an elder 'brother' whose reaction to similar frustrations has been as open and aggressive as his own has been secret and introspective, he comes alive in the classroom just once. This is when he is goaded by the mockery of his peers and the insistence of his teacher to reveal a passionate feeling for the kestrel he has trained and on which he spends all his time and money.

The film, which ought to be regular, compulsory viewing

---

* Based closely on the excellent novel, *A Kestrel for a Knave*, by Barry Hines, Penguin, 1969.

for the student and teacher trainer alike, has been criticized for a tendency to over-parody or for a reliance upon stock characters and situations. Certainly it may be said to present in its purest form the kind of language environment – for example school assemblies where piety and fascist discipline appear inseparable – which quickly suppresses personal response and initiative and which consequently inhibits the learning of all but a submissive minority. Whether or not the staff are stereotypes, the film's fidelity to the school *as it appears to the child* is attested by the reaction of schoolchildren viewing it. No one, observing them in the cinema, can doubt that they *recognize* the situations and attitudes portrayed. As for Billy Casper himself, anyone who has taught a class of fourth-year leavers will have met him, many times.

Billy is not found only in the leavers' sets, however, nor in the remedial classes, but in every situation where we have conveyed, explicity or by implication, the message that the pupil's experience is irrelevant. 'Boredom' is not the worst enemy, nor 'relevance' the best answer. The ultimate inhibitor of learning is that undervaluation of the individual implicit in the traditional tendency for the teacher to notice, above all – and perhaps exclusively, what a child *can't do*.

Appendix 1

**Part of a Discussion of Failure by Four Girls in a
Secondary Modern School**

After a fourth-year class had heard an extract from a short story
about a Welsh boy failing the 'eleven plus' from a BBC 'Speak'
programme, they split into groups and went away to talk it
over. I am indebted for the transcript to the student who was
teaching them at the time, Mrs Jenny Lloyd. I have also included
her comments, which add to the interest of the whole; she was a
good listener and she knew the pupils concerned. (These girls
were in fact from an 'A' stream. This shows perhaps in the level
of competence, but I have known much less able pupils *sustain*
a conversation almost as well and derive similar benefit from it.)

A I think it's a pity if ... the teachers expect you to do something then you fail ... it's a pity isn't it 'cos I mean they ...
   shouldn't expect you ... you know ... keep drumming into
   you that you could pass.

B If they think you're good enough ... to do something ...
   they sort of let you know exactly what ... well if they think
   you're going to pass an O-level say in English and they
   think you ought to ... I don't think they ought to push you
   ... you know ... 'cos you know yourself that you want to
   pass something and if you've got somebody going on at you
   all the time saying they want you to pass, you must do it, it
   doesn't make you do it any better (yes).

A I don't think you ought ... to be pushed on to do well as
   your brothers or your sisters (oh no). I think that's an awful
   pity because I mean not everybody in the family is going to
   be bright.

C No ... nobody's bright in our family ! (laughter)

D Oh ... what d'you do !

B No, but with my brother got into college now ... at least he will be and the trouble is Dad and Mum pushing me . . . not exactly . . . but they make it out . . . 'cos they say you've got more natural ability than Paul . . . so it shouldn't be so hard for you and I . . . so I don't believe that anyway . . . I think . . . I know . . . it could if I let it make me think . . . you know . . . I wanted to do as well as he . . . but I don't think that because . . .

A Well I wouldn't want to . . .

B No 'cos . . .

A I wouldn't want to be working purely for the fact that I wanted to do better than Hanna.

B I'd like to do as well as Paul but . . . I mean . . . If I don't that wouldn't bother me . . . if I did better it wouldn't bother him (no). No . . . because . . . we just say . . . I mean . . Oh glad you got on all right.

Speaker B, is finding it hard to express her feelings about her brother's success. Perhaps it is something hard to admit to the others. Then speaker A comes out forthrightly saying that she wouldn't want to be working *purely* to do better than her sister. Now speaker B can admit that she'd like to do as well as her brother, but it's not the end of the world if she doesn't.

They are helping each other along. This continues straight on:

A I don't think . . . Hanna she didn't do all that well at all . . . and I don't think Mum expects me to do any better . . . not really . . . and I think that's good and I don't want to . . . and I'd really worry about I would . . .

B I can't understand why people get worried sick over the fact that their sister's got about two or three O-levels more than you. I think if parents sort of say — You've got to do better than her . . . and put the fear of god into you, you're bound to . . . I think it's wrong to do that.

C Kath didn't get any O-levels.

A Didn't she?

B But she's got a job.

A Then she's got a job . . . I mean . . . she's got a fine job hasn't she?

C And then Brian got one whatever it was . . .

A Brian did pretty well.

C But then Mum's probably expecting me to do . . . you know
   . . . if I don't get anything she won't say . . .

A Go on.

They don't think parents should pressurize and they feel that
people who worry about brother's or sister's success are mistaken,
and yet they have their own worries and fears here, especially
over what Mum will say. . . . They know that you can get a
good job without great academic success. By sharing their fears
they are more able to meet them.

B I think in that tape we heard about parents and guardians I
   think it can be worse if they aren't exactly your parents (yes)
   because if it's an aunt or an uncle and they're looking after
   you . . .

A Why don't you say something Elizabeth?

B What was I saying . . . oh yes . . . I think it's worse if it's your
   guardian because you think you owe them something more
   than your parents . . . don't you (yes). Your parents look
   after you . . . but I mean that's their duty to sort of do everything (yes) and they've got more right to want you to do
   things than any guardian or anything . . . I think it's awful
   if somebody's always nagging on at you and that . . .

There is a strong feeling that parents have an inalienable right
over their children – more than 'any guardian'. That is very
strongly worded; the interpolated 'yes's' are strong reinforce-
ments of the feeling. One of them has clearly expressed the view
of all of them. Yet it's 'awful if somebody's always nagging on
at you and that . . .' This thought leads directly on to memories
of the eleven plus.

A I remember down (name of primary school) . . . you know
   we didn't have the eleven plus . . . we had several exams to do
   over a period of about six months . . . we didn't . . . I mean
   . . . we were so thick . . . I'd just sort of mess around. I wasn't
   bothered I never expected to go to the grammar school . . . I
   never wanted to so I didn't mind.

D I didn't mind, but when I knew ...

B I didn't mind it was the fact that we knew we weren't exactly intelligent ... Dad* just sort of said that they were exams and they'd count you know, but it wasn't exactly eleven plus. And we didn't know when we were going to take them. We'd just say 'Oh, we're going to have exams today' and it was awful ... because I always seemed to have an awful cold when it came to exams. You know when you've got a cold ... when you've got a really bad cold ... and all stuffed up all the time, you never do as well. But – um – what I didn't like was that they weren't sure about me or something. I wasn't one thing or the other. This man came to interview me. He was really horrible (oh yes). He spent about half an hour ...

C In your Dad's office ...

A Why did he interview you?

B Well, I suppose I was borderline or something (oh). What I didn't like was that he ... I felt awful because when I'd done it I didn't know whether I'd done well or badly and we sort of waited for the results ... and Dad sort of said 'Could you come in and speak to Mr S'. ... So I went in his office and he looked at me as if ... as if I don't know whether it was ... because I was sort of Dad's daughter and everything (yes) but he just ... he was really nasty, because he ... um ... he sort of expected you ... he said ... you know ... which do you consider your worst subject. I said maths, or arithmetic. He said 'Oh!, I thought spelling was'. Well ... what does spelling mean? It is a bit stupid – it puts you off ... I mean you can get by without it. Well at the end he said 'Let's have a go at some of your arithmetic.' So he did and said 'Oh, I know what you mean.' (Ooh, cheek, blimey). And he said 'It's about time you thought about work instead of horses all the time.'

A Ooh, he didn't!

B And he made me feel I was a failure anyway and I knew

* Her father is a headmaster.

after that that I hadn't passed and when Dad told me, you know ... I felt really awful.

D I didn't mind if I didn't pass 'cos my Mum was always telling me not to worry about it ... But when he told me he said that there was five that passed out of the twenty ... like ... I just didn't think it was me and I was even more disappointed when they said, but you know you get over it ... you feel a bit of a failure and when you have to go and tell Mum ... you know ...

A Oh ... we had a letter and it said ...

C You knew it was coming 'cos they'd always keep you behind in the break and he was telling ... ugh ...

A I was ever so pleased when I was coming to (name of secondary school). I always fancied ... 'cos ... you ... see ... Hanna'd been here and I thought – Oh good ...

C I was pleased that I was going somewhere different from Ruth (yes).

D I thought I'd hate it ...

Speaker A never expected to go to the grammar school, so couldn't be disappointed when she didn't go. She is emphatically pleased to be going to the secondary modern. Speaker D says she didn't mind but adds the elliptical 'but when I knew ...' She reinforces this further on by saying she thought she'd hate the secondary modern. Speaker B also has a proviso to her 'didn't mind'. She minded a lot and goes on to relate the unhappy experience of her borderline interview. This made the process of failing more painful. Speaker B's speech about the interview is studded with incomplete sentences, restarted and never finished; many 'you know's' and repetitions. All indicative of her difficulty in relating the incident. Yet she is better for having been able to share it with sympathetic friends. All the girls pick up the cruel sarcasm of Mr S in their support for speaker B.

B Ah, let me think – never been top of the class ...

A Well, we don't have it, do we? Some classes have it where you're numbered, you know.

C That's what they do at ...

B I don't feel it any more you know, but I did 'cos we always used to be top didn't we? (yes). Me and Teresa and you, we always ... we were all sort of ... in the first and second year we were like it. I don't think we did after that. But I still used to get top ... quite high marks ... but not with my maths though ... I was disappointed with them ... I sort of thought I'd failed after always getting good marks and then now practically always getting bad marks. But I don't think I deserve to get bad marks all the time (no).

A No, I mean ... of course you do ...

C When you do a good piece of work ...

A I think you know if you're going to get a good mark.

D Sometimes Lynn did good stuff ... didn't she ... but didn't get good marks for it.

C Disappointing when you hand in a piece of work and you think it's good and when you get it back you've got a low mark (yes).

B Sometimes now ... not quite so much ... but sometimes I feel I've done a good piece of work and I feel I don't know when I get it back you know ... and I've really tried. And you don't get a good mark and when you sort of feel ... oh I forgot to do my work and you do it (yes) quickly, and you get good marks (yeah).

A You get marks ... I just can't understand it ...

When speaking about success, especially recent success, there seems to be an increase in the hesitation and there are many incomplete sentences. This perhaps indicates the difficulty in admitting success, but it is good for people to know when they have done something well. It indicates a degree of self-evaluation. Speaker B thinks she knows when she's done a good piece of work and is puzzled when others don't agree. But at least she can say to her friends ... ' ... I've done a good piece of work,' though she has to preface this with 'sometimes now ... not quite so much ... but sometimes I feel ...'

Appendix 2

Curriculum Examples

*The Family**

Although this school did not have a fully integrated course, nevertheless from time to time it devoted a concentrated block of work to areas of inquiry within the scope of such a course. The area of inquiry described here occupied the whole of three consecutive weeks' teaching time normally used for the separate disciplines of English, history, geography and religious education, and was in operation for the whole of a fourth-year group. The preparation involved the headmaster and the senior teachers of each subject as well as all the teachers taking part. The plan was to use team-teaching techniques so that most of the introductory material was used for the whole range and presented by the specialists. For the follow-up work the year divided into five or more small seminar groups each with their own teacher. The area of inquiry chosen for this report is 'The Family' which may well figure in many humanities courses, although not every school will necessarily wish to develop the work this way.

Basically the work was divided into two main time approaches:

1. The structure, function and purpose of the family in:
(a) Tribal situation
(b) Middle Ages
(c) Industrial Revolution
(d) The early twentieth century

2. The changes, and reasons for these changes, in the family since grandfather was a boy:
(a) External influence:
i   Industrial expansion
ii Communications (cars, roads, mass media)

*Schools Council (1967, pp. 6–9).

iii Spending patterns and wages
iv The welfare state
v Education

(b) Effect of 2 (a) on the internal structure of the family with particular reference to:

i Women at work
ii Early marriage
iii Decline in authority of 'father'
iv Teenage culture

In 2 (a) the influences were examined in the general situation, in 2 (b) the approach was more personal.

Supporting material was prepared in advance by the school and consisted of:

1. A brief definition of the four requisites for family structure:
(a) A married couple
(b) Children of this relationship
(c) Provision for the care, protection and education of these children within the family
(d) Common residence to fulfil economic, social and educative needs

The typical family was represented by:

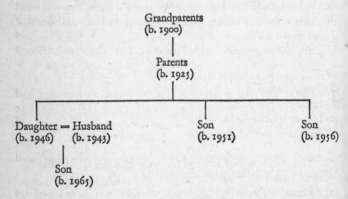

2. A preliminary outline of the basic information each teacher would require. This discussed the anthropological basis of the 'family' in prehistoric times, problems of polygamy as

illustrated by the story of Abraham, reasons for polygamy. A report on attempts to suppress the family as a social unit. A summary of English family life in the main periods of part I with supporting evidence and quotations.

3. Detailed broadsheets on individual assignments in both parts I and 2. These were for use in seminars and for homework which was part of the work each week. For example, the broadsheets for part I contained:

(a) Accounts of family life in New Guinea and Samoa.

(b) A list of chattels left by a certain man who died in 1300, and an account of the activities of the wife and sister of John Paston, a landowner. These illustrated and contrasted living conditions in people of different class and also emphasized the place of women in the family during the Middle Ages, as well as the financial implications of marriage.

(c) The family life of the Industrial Revolution was illustrated in greater detail by quotations from many sources and from statistics of the times. For example, a Frenchman who visited England in 1871, wrote: 'The street boys swarm, more repulsive than the scum in Paris; without question the climate is worse and the gin more deadly. Families have been discovered with no bed other than a heap of soot; there is but one refuge – drunkenness.' And the housewife in York who said 'if there's anything extra to buy, such as a pair of boots for one of the children, me and the children goes without dinner, but Jim (her husband) takes 'is dinner to work and I give it 'im as usual. 'E never knows we go without, and I never tells 'im.'

(d) The family of the 1900s was even better documented and the account of the clothes worn by a young lady of the time could not fail to interest (and appal!) the modern miss of today.

Each of these broadsheets was supported by illustrations and backed by a questionnaire. For example:

1. Make a list of all different relatives you have who are blood relatives with you. Then compare this list with one for either your mother or your father. What differences do you notice?

2. How much are you expected to look after younger brothers and sisters? Do you think that older children should help to look after younger ones?

3. Do you think that today a man and his wife should share his wages equally? Should a man pay his wife for her work in the home? Who should pay for the house and furniture when a young couple are just starting up?

4. In what ways should a child be encouraged to remain childish, and for how long? How grown up should you be when you enter this (secondary) school and when you leave?

Duplicated forms were provided for the statistical questions and also for a survey of family life today, based on the family life of the boys and girls. Two of the films which were used for group showing were *The Goddess* (BFI) and *Four Families* (Gas Council). These opened the way for a discussion of the problems created in our modern society within a family. Other supporting working papers provided information in detail on the changing nature of industry and its effect on the family; one particular paper was partially based on George Orwell's *The Road to Wigan Pier* and others described the impact on family life of the motor car and of TV.

In the third week the group turned to the study of a particular family, 'The Wood Family', the purpose of the work being to show how greatly things have changed since grandfather's day. The family was a local one. Grandfather had worked as a cooper in the local brewery. Father was a semi-skilled machine operator on shift work in a local paper mill. He had had a spell in the army and now lives on a new estate in the town. The married daughter has a flat in a town some fifteen miles away, her husband is a grocer's roundsman. Mother has been working since her youngest son started school.

The material includes a small drama written around an incident in the Wood family house at 6.30 in the evening. This involves a typical family conflict over homework and TV, children being out when their father expects them home and the 'when I was a lad things were different' attitude of the father to the sons.

After the play was over, discussion groups considered the points it had made. These included the position of women at work, the decline in the status of the father, earlier marriage and teenage culture, all of which were worked out in full with notes prepared for the teachers. The film, *The Goddess*, was also used in this part of the course.

In conclusion it may be said that this school had acted as its own development centre for this three-week exercise, that it had realized the value of a team-teaching approach and made sure that beforehand all the teachers involved were fully informed from the beginning so that adequate material was prepared. Wherever possible it appealed to personal experience and by taking the family for its area of inquiry, it had chosen a course which was of immediate interest to the boys and girls and which was of real importance for their future.

Note on the school

This is a new, mixed, secondary modern school (550-600 pupils), which serves a post-war housing estate, almost entirely council housing, on the edge of a large town in southern England. The school has new buildings which are not overcrowded. The English and Humanities Department are organized by experienced heads of department, although there is a high turnover rate in assistant staff.

Nearly 50 per cent of the age group stay at school for a fifth year, and each year about ten or a dozen pupils remain in the sixth form.

The number of pupils taking the course described above is 130, the entire fourth year. They are taught in forms of twenty-five to thirty. Seminar groups consist of fifteen to twenty pupils. The number of teachers directly involved is six to eight, all specialists in geography or history or religious education. Five to seven periods a week are allotted to the course, which lasts a month, and the periods are divided into double periods or blocks.

This is a new scheme. It is being extended during 1966-7 and incorporated in the normal working of the timetable as part of a compulsory social-science course.

Example 2

This is part of the Humanities Curriculum Project sponsored jointly by the Schools Council and the Nuffield Foundation.

This material on the Family is one of several collections intended for use with fourteen to sixteen year olds of average or below average ability and which can either be used as a separate 'subject' on the timetable or as a core for the integration of traditional subjects. Schools that have timetabled it separately have tended to allocate to it five or six periods per week and at least two teachers. Fuller accounts of the project may be found in the *Journal of Curriculum Studies,* vol. 1, no. 1, November 1968; *New Society,* 24 July 1969 and *The Humanities Curriculum Project: Interim Report,* 1969, Schools Council Publications Company.

Each of the topics or areas of inquiry has a handbook for the teacher which contains a brief introduction and an extensive index, not only of the broadsheets but also of other material, including film. What follows is the explanatory part of the handbook for the material on 'The Family'* together with two randomly chosen pages of the index. These I hope will give some idea of the range and variety of the broadsheets that are available.

The Family

The Family would seem to have immediate relevance as a topic for inquiry with adolescents: they will all bring some kind of personal experience to it.

At the same time this will create tensions and areas of extreme sensitivity, since the texture of family life will be infinitely varied. And in many groups there will be pupils who have not been reared by their natural parents; orphans, adopted children, children of broken homes, children brought up by relatives other than their parents. There will also be some illegitimate children.

One hopes that it will be possible for pupils to take an objective look at the family as a group; assess its structure and effectiveness in different settings, probe its relationships, and come to a deeper understanding of the whole concept of *family*.

---

*Quotations are from the *first* version, edited by Maurice Plaskow. The version currently marketed by Heinemann differs slightly in layout but not in substance.

The material has therefore been selected to provide wide-ranging points of view of the role of family, and studies and experience of diverse family situations. Some of the material derives from very unfamiliar settings to provide an opportunity for exploring a range of social structure and *mores*.

Some of the settings nearer home will also reflect a style of life which will be outside many children's personal experiences. There is evidence supporting the permanent need for the strength of the family unit. There is evidence criticizing the institution of the family, and questioning its survival. Thus it ought to be possible for children not living with their parents to derive support for the advantages of their situation, rather than having a sense of deprivation reinforced.

It is difficult to see that an inquiry could succeed unless a fundamental appraisal were made, which allowed a divergence of view to emerge in any group which had made a considerable exploration.

We would offer a word of caution about the injection of the pupils' personal situations.

In a topic as sensitive as the *family* teachers will obviously use their judgement and close knowledge of their pupils to avoid causing embarrassment and possible upset by asking pupils to give details of their own family. Obviously problems and tensions will emerge, either directly, or in role-plays or personal writing and art work. But there will be a delicate line between insight and dismay.

Teachers will need all the time to bear in mind that they may have accepted a range of values which are unfamiliar to many of their pupils. It is important not to register surprise or disbelief through tone or gesture, and to allow the evidence to depersonalize the case.

Selection and structure

The material in the collection now offered has been selected from a very large amount with an attempt to provide as wide a range of opinion and experience as possible at a level which most pupils will be able to apprehend, if not fully comprehend.

There has been a careful attempt not to build in bias; there are no right or wrong answers; one hopes that pupils will be able to find some support for any value position they are led to or wish to explore.

Inevitably a great many interesting topics have been forced out in the final selection, and teachers and pupils will have to search for their own evidence at many points.

One is torn between a scanty coverage and a more extended justice to fewer, major areas.

Teachers may not agree on the final selection; we shall be interested to receive comments on the balance as it appears, with suggestions for more effective treatment of the theme, given the limitations within which we are all forced to work.

The structure which has been chosen was mainly a convenience for the gathering of material, and should not be considered a fixed route. Since the material appears roughly grouped the broad areas are given in the next section, but teachers will find a more extensive cross-referencing of the material under a variety of headings in order to help greater flexibility of use.

It would certainly be inadvisable to work one's way steadily through the collection, as though it were a textbook!

As with other packs visuals are included, in this case numbered in with the rest of the material: some photographed in black and white, a few in the form of colour slides, where it has been possible to obtain reproductions of paintings. There are also tape recordings, both of material which occurs in the pack in written form, and other extracts which exist only in audio form.

There is a separate list of films selected and annotated to make a contribution to the inquiry.

The main areas

The material has been gathered under four main headings:

1. Structure
2. Roles
3. Kinship
4. Controls

1. *Structure* There are examples of different family units, both in this country and elsewhere, and a fair amount of sociological material on the nature and function of the family.

Teachers may feel it inappropriate to start with an abstract consideration of the nature of the family, but will want to link this with examples in more concrete form of the way people live together. The cross-referencing will help – but there is no substitute for a thorough acquaintance with the material. . . .

2. *Roles* Charts the stances of husband and wife and members of the family.
The changing role of women, and the consequent effects on their husbands.
Attitudes towards marriage; family size.
Illegitimacy and adoption.
Attitudes towards child-rearing and education.

3. *Kinship* Concentrates on the relationship between immediate members of the family:

parents and children, children with each other;

then relationships with the rest of the family, particularly the changing role of grandparents and parents-in-law.

4. *Controls* are considered under three main topics:

(a) economics

(b) divorce

(c) religion

One of the reasons why the material has not been tightly separated into separate questions or headings is that it will be obviously difficult to delineate those factors which affect the quality of family life and relationships. Economics and environment may well have an effect on kinship, as will divorce and religion. Attitudes to child-rearing will again be affected by social pressures, education, religion and environment.

Family: The Material – Synopsis (two typical pages)

1. *Heredity*: short poem by Thomas Hardy (1840–1928) A reflection on the continuance of man through generations of the family.

   *

2. *Universality of the family*: short extract from *The Family and Marriage in Britain* by Ronald Fletcher.

3. *The family must be abolished*: short extract from Plato's *Republic*.

4. *Aspects of kinship*: extract from *Communities in Britain* by Ronald Frankenburg. Comment on kinship lines, extended families and kinship differences.

5. *Variations in the family*: extract from the *Family in Various Cultures* by Queen, Haberstein and Adams. Contrast between our nuclear families and different units in other cultures.

6. *The extended family*: extract from *The Family and Social Change* by Rosser and Harris. Comment on the linguistic use of the word *family*.

7. *Some questions on the nature of the modern family*: extract from *The Family and Marriage in Britain* by Ronald Fletcher. A comprehensive list of questions on the present condition of the family and influences being brought to bear upon it.

8. *An anti-family note in western culture*: short extract from *Sociology* by W. J. H. Sprott. The effects on the family of the welfare state.

   *Each item is printed on a separate sheet or sheets.

Appendix 3

Drama

In a matter of perhaps twenty years drama has grown from what many saw as a somewhat outlandish optional extra until it now occupies a recognized place in even the secondary curriculum, though its hold here – in the grammar school especially – is less secure than at infant level, where it is virtually impregnable. All this should not be taken to imply a single meaning for a term which may cover very disparate activities. Drama may mean:

1. *Mime,* a form which, partly because of the absence of speech places a particular emphasis on concentration and physical control. It has a special appeal for pre-adolescents and also for those relatively inarticulate pupils for whom the freedom from the demands of speech represents a real liberation and a new opportunity for self-expression. At the same time mime offers a real discipline for it depends upon a concentrated recollectedness in which the pupil rediscovers his own experience and also perceives more acutely the behaviour of others. In this process ideas are formulated and crystallized in ways which, though first expressed in mime, may become evident in various aspects of English to which mime may be easily linked.

2. *Dramatic movement;* this often appears in the primary curriculum as 'music and movement' and aims at the development of physical control and awareness in conjunction with an increased sensitivity to sound and rhythm. Where the dramatic element is stressed it moves towards

3. *Dance-drama,* which is gaining in popularity in work with adolescents, who find the response to music fits in naturally with their interest in pop and for whom the freedom from the demands of speech, coupled with vivid physical sensation, is particularly liberating.

4. *Improvisation,* involving the spontaneous working through of dramatic situations based upon their own experience, or upon themes suggested by plays, films, novels, newspaper accounts, etc. Improvisation increases awareness of other people's behaviour, including quite specifically the way they speak. Not only this, under a competent teacher many normally inarticulate adolescents discover that the playing of roles frees them from customary inhibitions. In such situations their fluency confirms that they possess unsuspected language resources which can emerge in an unstressed 'play' situation but are otherwise stifled as a result of social conditioning processes they have undergone. Because of the ways it promotes awareness and the recovery of pure zest, improvisation is now increasingly used in conjunction with, or in preparation for work on

5. *Dramatic texts;* these will mostly be the work of familiar authors but there is also a place for the script written by pupils themselves (often after improvisation).

6. *Radio drama;* for school purposes, this provides an opportunity to concentrate upon oral confidence and the increasingly adventurous use of the voice. There are various tasks to be performed by the non-vocal or the technically minded pupils, and the work is not seriously hampered by the restrictions of a conventional classroom.

This is by no means an exhaustive list. Most drama teachers use methods which combine a number of these and other elements but the main emphasis is now normally placed upon self-expression as opposed to dramatic art-forms. Self-expression however should not be taken to imply an egotistical obsession with one's own traumatic experiences but a process in which awareness of self both complements and is dependent upon an increasing sensitivity towards others. Finally, it must be emphasized that work in drama provides a facilitating atmosphere for almost every kind of talk – expressive, reflective, planning, evaluative – and is in turn enriched by it.

A measure of the growing influence of drama is the simple fact that those who continue to deny it a place nowadays feel bound to justify their position. Nor does the debate stop there; there is increasing support for the inclusion of drama in the curriculum of colleges of education, both as an expressive activity in its own right and as conductive to greater confidence, sensitivity and flexibility in the professional performance of teachers. To take but one example, I have a colleague who finds dance-drama invaluable in the training of maths graduates!

These emotional aspects are particularly relevant when one is considering the place of drama in work with children who are culturally and linguistically deprived. A considerable number of the personal characteristics of disadvantaged children which were listed in chapter three (p. 76) can be considerably modified through drama. In order to support this contention I shall comment on several groups of these characteristics and endeavour to show some of the effects upon them of work in drama.

Personal characteristics modifiable through drama
Substitutes aggressive action for aggressive language; poor physical coordination.

If one visits a school for specially handicapped children one can see clear signs of the physical tension that arises through the frustration of inarticulateness. In conventional schools the same frustration is present, though to a lesser degree, and it is exacerbated by the restrictions on the release of physical energy. In *Roaring Boys* (1966), Edward Blishen painted a vivid picture of the cramping conditions, the classroom where tiny desks were perched on huge knees. The traditional answer, providing an outlet for physical energy on the playing field in team games, is increasingly seen to serve the needs of only a minority. It is not just that sport in this sense is sufficiently individualized; the very concept of 'team' in terms of self-subordination to a group is often foreign to the child from a deprived background. The drama room permits physical excitement and the liberation of physical energy makes other kinds of liberation progressively more feasible. It is significant that with PE, certainly at primary level, the development has been away from drill towards more individualized, experimental and even imaginative activities. Here, as in the drama room, the pace is not prescribed and the individual can develop the confidence that must precede the achievement of better physical control. Just as in a workshop situation (see p. 154) this means not the end of teaching but the beginning of a teaching that can be effective since it is built on a professional appreciation of the needs of individual children. The sceptic should watch the performance of fat, adolescent girls in the hands of a sensitive teacher of modern dance. The weakness of much PE work nevertheless seems to me to lie in its still affording insufficient scope for individual *expression*. It is as hopeless to expect disadvantaged girls to be motivated by concepts like 'good' or 'pure movement' as by those concepts that relate to the playing of hockey or netball.

Aimless activity.
Susceptible to peer-group rather than adult pressure.
Concentration severely limited.
Functions badly in activities of the imagination.

The conventional curriculum in both its content and its language has remained external and alien to the disadvantaged child; it has failed to present either explicitly or implicitly aims that are feasible or even comprehensible. In such a situation a baffled child 'looks' aimless and lacking in concentration. Moreover the behaviour of adults in the teaching environment is such as to reinforce his reliance upon the support of his peers. I have mentioned already, however, that the immature adolescent may not enjoy trying to 'keep up with' his contemporaries. Hence such a situation is likely to intensify that behaviour which we, teachers, characterize as 'aimless'.

In these circumstances drama may be effective firstly, simply as a situation in which some aimlessness is *permitted*; the adolescent, under pressure from all sides to grow up, may value it simply as a breathing space. It is valuable too in providing activities in which 'the childish' and 'the adult' are not explicitly differentiated: it may be quite comfortable, in the drama room for once, to be childish. This kind of motivation seems to lie behind the release which apparently tough, modern adolescents find in entering a very un-modern world of myth and legend, elemental forces of good and evil operating in lands where demons are a commonplace. The broad symbols can be invested for every individual with his own meanings and preoccupations. At the same time, as confidence grows, his reliance upon his peers fits naturally into a situation where he is expected to cooperate with them, as he was in the English workshop. In the same way too, the working together leads to the use of the teacher as a resource, and discussion and evaluation of issues far wider than the drama rooms inevitably follow – why do people act like that? In those circumstances, what would you do? In the early stages, before cooperation develops, the imagination will occasionally have been deeply stirred, and now in the discussion it will be constantly called upon in the effort to interpret behaviour.

Self-effacing.
Expects and accepts failure.
Possesses no accomplishments.
Lack of initiative in response.

The first of these may obviously be a reaction to that predicament where the child's behaviour appears aimless – where he is torn between an aggressive peer culture and the largely incomprehensible demands that 'school' makes upon him. In his Walsall working paper John Dixon suggested that the introverted child, reacting to a harsh existence, pins his faith on submissiveness in such a way that we have to try art and drama as fresh areas in which we have a real chance of encouraging him to discover or, as Dixon says, 'assert *himself*' – self-effacement is but one aspect of the way he expects and – sadder still – he accepts failure. It is, of course, true that a really disadvantaged child presents the appearance of being good at nothing, and certainly the myth that providence compensated the child for intellectual underdevelopment by making him 'practical' or giving him big muscles has long been exploded. Nevertheless the depressing picture to *some* extent is the product of our point of view. Here the importance of the drama situation is that it provides a context in which failure is no longer a relevant concept. Informal group situations in drama lead pupils to respond to each other and so, gradually, they learn to respond with new initiative to the teacher. Paradoxically, precisely because they have been able to respond *by not responding*, and have seen this *accepted,* positive response becomes more and more natural.

Chapter three included a list not only of personal characteristics some of which we have just considered but, more specifically, of nineteen language habits of disadvantaged children. On nine of these, set out below, drama may be expected to make some impact:

Speaks haltingly without physical defect.
Speaks often in monotone.
Indiscriminate in both noisy and quiet responses.
Seldom or never asks questions.
Cause and effect relationships absent in speech.
Rarely engages in dialogue with adults.
Talks almost exclusively about things.
Unable to vary language with situation.
Reluctant to move from oral to written language.

By now enough has been implied about the way drama 'works' to make detailed comment on these superfluous. Summarizing, however, one would say that the drama situation, with its emphasis upon acceptance and cooperative endeavour, is one where the faults of lack of confidence or control are remedied because they are not highlighted with every utterance, and because enjoyable experimentation, for its own sake, is encouraged. As soon as the group engages actively upon a narrative theme, moreover, the planning that is involved necessitates thinking about cause and effect, about people's behaviour and their language in different situations; question-asking of one's peers becomes entirely natural and soon the teacher too is involved.

After this rather clinical examination of the effects of drama, the following extract from the Department of Education and Science report on drama conveys something of the texture of the work itself. The fact that it relates to work in the primary school may usefully emphasize the foundations upon which the secondary school should build. Equally important, it is specifically concerned with the effect of drama work upon children's *language*:

The use of language

We were particularly interested in the course of our survey to find examples of work in improvised drama having given rise to the interesting use of language spoken and written. We should emphasize, in giving examples, that in improvised drama the use of words is only part of what is, or should be, a total expression of a situation. Words divorced from their context can sound crude. Reduced to the printed page they lack the tension, the emotion, the excitement with which they were originally uttered and which were a part of their original quality. An example of this occurred at a school in a London borough. A third-year class had pushed back the desks and in the few square feet that were clear in front of the blackboard they improvised a cross-channel swim with a bland and observant radio commentator. There were five English supporters at Dover and fifteen French for the interesting reason that the children found 'magnifique' more fun to yell than 'hurrah'. They then went on to give an improvisation of the last act of Richard III in which every kind of imprecation was heaped on the unlucky king. The climactic words were 'May you have his liver for breakfast!' Some may think this phrase hardly worthy of quotation and when we add that the whole thing was done with wooden swords, balaclavas, and saucepan lids for shields, some may say that this confirms their worst suspicions of classroom drama. But there are two important aspects of this work that must be considered before any judgement is made. The first, in the usual words, is 'what is it doing for the children?' and secondly, 'what is it doing for them in the future?' In answering the first question it is difficult to avoid the phrases commonly used to justify drama such as it frees the children'. More accurately this kind of work might be said to make possible the total involvement of the children in an imaginative situation, and just as a skilful teacher can use children's involuntary dramatic play for all kinds of valuable educational experiences, so she can use an episode of this kind, containing so strong an ingredient of play, as a basis for further educational activities of which writing may well be one of the most important. Examples of written work arising out of drama are given below.

The answer to the second question, that concerning the future of the children, was answered when we visited the top juniors who had had experience of drama throughout their time at this school. In a small space in front of the blackboard they gave a pretty faithful version of the story of Macbeth. There was an element of play in their work, but at the same time they were beginning to act a play. They made clear that they knew a very great deal about the play and found real sense in arguing out the situations and exploring the nature of the characters in their own way and their own words.

I often wonder what's inside those rebel heads.'
Send the men to the jousting!'
This banquet is too good of you.'
Nothing is too good for you. You are my king.'

'Murder Duncan? But I always thought women were gentle people.'
'Now you know.'

And the leader of the eight exceedingly vigorous witches, having dismissed Macbeth with the prophecy that his heirs should not be king, said:

'Ladies, let us retire to our stew.'

A further example of the remarkable ability of children to grasp a dramatic situation and to express it in their own words comes from a school in the north-east. It is situated in a somewhat impoverished area and with few exceptions the academic ability of the children is low. The top class had been working for some weeks on the story of the plague in the Derbyshire village of Eyam in the seventeenth century. The theme had something in common with *The Crucible* though it was in no way derivative. It concerned the identity of a thief in the village, a woman accused of being a witch, the death of her son, and the poisoning of the water in the village well. After a short talk with the head, the children worked for forty minutes on this theme with one short interruption. Then they had to be stopped as it was break.

These children showed an extraordinary ability to grasp every element of a fairly complex situation and to work out the relationships of a great variety of characters to each other and to the central situation. They were able to pick up the lead from each other so that the action was advanced not by inventing new action but by exploring more widely, and so in greater depth, the reactions of the people in the village to the central situation, that of witchcraft. Their language was rich and fluent though the drive with which it was delivered and the thick lilting dialect in which it was uttered made it impossible to take down. They were quite assured in using the space provided by a large hall, avoided bunching or straggling, preserved the relationship between the groups and the individual characters, and were economical but expressive in their movements. Here are some examples of what they wrote in their classroom in connection with the play.

From a girl of average intelligence: 'The world is tilting upside down and spinning fast and I am dizzy and my gums are swelling. My stomach is upset and I feel lumps beneath my arms and legs.'

This passage was hardly decipherable:
'I am in the village and I have got the plague. I wear charms round my neck to protect me. I went to church and said my prayers. I went to Margaret the witch and she gave me potions and spells and I put signs on my door but I have the plague. I lie in bed with the door o

my house locked and a red cross painted on the door. Lord have mercy on us!'

And from an eight year old:
'And each time they nod their faces at the sign of no.'

It is important to be clear about this. In some schools teachers may find that the children can write as vividly as that without the stimulus of drama. But the head of this school says that he finds drama a way of helping his children not only to express themselves in words but to think. And the outstanding quality of the children's work in drama was indeed its intelligence. They could express their penetration in spoken and written language (Department of Education and Science, 1968, pp. 11–13)

Such an account inevitably makes memories of secondary-school drama seem incredibly formal and limited. At primary level there is no problem of separate learning compartments. At secondary level the link between English and drama is partly a matter of content, partly of situation. Dramatists have long been studied among the texts for literature examinations. The connection now proposed is more fundamental, however. Along with other literature, drama – so far from merely providing a special kind of text for study or analysis – is to be harnessed to a continuing process of self-discovery that is a particular concern of the English teacher. One defines one's own identity not in an introspective vacuum, but in a social setting; the extent to which I know myself is very much dependent on my awareness of other people. To encourage this process is to provide both motivation and context not just for development towards some vague goal like 'social-adjustment' but for the fuller and more precise articulation of feeling and thought – in other words for the development of precisely those social and verbal competencies that society demands. While we build upon personal experience its limitations are apparent and we see self-awareness being refined and extended by the experience of a literature that is full of people worth knowing.

To emphasize, as I have, the social element in self-discovery is not to deny the importance of privacy, or the chance to be one-self. Paradoxically, this is quite feasible within the social context of drama work. Some kinds of drama and movement work enable the individual to be essentially on his own; through working with others, his introspections and self-discovery can remain as private as he desires. The atmosphere as well as specific types of work should be conducive to essential privacies. It is not merely that in the drama room the option to withdraw and do nothing should be a real one; the presence of others, if they trust the teacher enough to be themselves, helps rather than inhibits. Thus the drama room becomes an oasis where the child can unobtrusively cherish that one of his various personalities that seems important at that time.

As I have argued, the whole process can only begin in a classroom atmosphere which admits of more flexible roles than merely teacher and taught, and which by its openness and warmth fosters as many kinds of verbal and non-verbal activity as possible. Even though from a traditionalist point of view such a classroom appears disorganized, it can with careful planning and organization, place a new emphasis upon cooperative modes of working. The value of the activities is now intrinsic, not dependent upon some end-product: the taping of an interview, for example, is a situation in which talk, listening, planning and evaluation go on, and these count for more than the final tape itself. The same is true of the making of a film, as this account of a project with a random group of thirty-two third formers makes clear:

Every one of the thirty-two children had work to do, although I admit, some had more to do than others, and a few were watching for much of the time. But they did watch and from the wall came comment and criticism and advice. On leaving school that evening after first shooting I ran into the mother of one of the shyest girls in the class. 'Hello, Mrs Parish, we started shooting our film today' – 'Yes, I know,' she replied 'Brenda hasn't stopped talking about it ever since she came into tea.'

What more justification do we need than such a comment, if we believe that the school's responsibility for the growth of language can be helped by providing experiences which capture the children's interest, and so engender a flow of natural talk.

In the next six or seven weeks of Thursday morning shootings I discovered what I feel to be the true role of the teacher. He is the producer, not the director; that is the teacher organizes the administration in relation to school affairs, supervises the overall control and finance and keeps an eye on the time. The detail of directing the film, choosing locations and giving advice to actors should be left to a child director. I only once looked through the viewfinder and that was only a check that the boy cameraman wouldn't fall off the parapet of a seventh storey balcony as he filmed the scene in action below! The teacher asks pertinent and awkward questions from the side and provokes continuous discussion. For the rest, he has faith and trust. Sometimes they filmed odd brief incidents after school and on those occasions they learnt to work by themselves.

As we walked through the streets and set to work on location we had to deal with public comment. 'I mean it's disgusting, all them kids roaming the street, they ought to be back in school doing some work. What's the modern school coming to. Here, teacher, what do you think you're up to?' So I was forced to consider what I was achieving. 'Doing some work?' What we came to realize is that many of the traditional values of school can be acquired and provided for in surprisingly different ways, and the wider the range of situation and demands that children experience, the more willing is the attention and concentration that they give. They would often spend up to an hour just getting one minute's worth of story filmed. If I rushed them they objected because I was breaking the concentrated rhythm of their own way of working. They spent one whole day at half term filming in a friend's house. But many of the people we met in the street, and especially the parents, were appreciative of what was being educated. In terms of prolonged concentration the time was considerable and the absorption and enthusiasm had to be sustained over four months. And after that, in the following autumn term, four boys undertook the cutting and editing of the film (not a form activity) for fifty consecutive lunch hours. How's that for stamina and perseverance!

The children had learnt to be resourceful; money was short, time was restricted and locations were limited. Yet they managed to negotiate with a rag and bone man to turn up at an agreed place and time with his horse and cart to take part in the film. Neither did it go smoothly: continuity was continually interrupted by the loss of some film, the setting of a vital property, the absence of children through illness or holiday, or mum throwing away the hero's striped shirt. And all these situations needed immediate solutions. The script was abandoned when it proved too cumbersome and the last part of the story was improvised on the spot which in many ways turned out to be the most effective part of the film.

Talk had been incessant throughout our time together; so much of it had been that tussling with language which clear communication of ideas and directions to others require. That others understood one's point now really mattered and hours were spent in argument and self-criticism. But then there had also been the relief of social banter and chat, so that the whole experience had given us a chance for growth in social ability and fluency. And not least had been what I as their teacher had found out about each of them as more fully realized individuals. A remark made by a teacher in their fourth year, when the film was finished and done with, related to this matter in social development; she noticed a distinctive style in the way they conducted themselves and got down to work.

Whether language had developed it's difficult to say. But it is perhaps worth noting that their written work later was especially interesting and sensitive. I would argue that the experience of making a film does educate a creative and dramatic sensibility and particularly evoke a visual awareness of the local world in which the children live. A group activity of this kind requires too that their response be total and unified; it must involve a response to places, people and ideas, together with a sense of criticism (Clements, 1967).

In all these situations the teacher has set up frameworks in which learning can take place, he is at hand to facilitate and instruct, but ideally he is learning too. Something of this climate comes over in the following account by Valerie Sexton, a graduate on teaching practice, of a session with a third-year secondary modern 'B' stream at a local 'theatre workshop'.

So, we arrive at the Workshop again, I've remembered the door key and the records. The kids are next door putting on their plimsolls. I wonder how they feel. I am struggling with the window blind and the lights as they drift in, in ones and twos and sit at the side of the room. I call them into a group in the centre. They wait for instructions.

'Now, quiet please, we don't want to waste any time. I want you to move around the room anywhere you like. It's Saturday night. You are going to a dance and you feel great. Talk to people you meet, say hello and let them see how good you feel.'

I started the record, the kids prance around, heads high. The hall resounds with the quick heavy beat; 'Tracey when I'm with you, something you do, bounces me off the ceiling'. Some pick up the beat in their walk, some boys adopt a slick clothes and 'King of the Swinger' swagger.

I wait for the record to end. This sort of activity must not last too long. Thirty-two get restless quickly and they already have expressed in discussions an impatience with any 'warming-up period', preferring to 'get down to it'.

I call the class together again and tell them to relax while I explain that what we are going to do connects with the story we had on Monday – Stan Barstow's *The Desperadoes* – I ask them to remember how alive and free Vince had felt when he was with Iris and then how he had felt during the fight with Jackson. (Once I have said this the connection does seem rather nebulous.) I ask them to move around the room again, but this time being afraid of something or someone following them. They are to use any part of their body in moving – not just legs, and to express fear on their faces. (I worry about whether I should have told them this or just see if it came naturally.) I play the James Bond theme, they respond excitedly to this music. When the record finishes, I demonstrate fighting motions, throwing the whole weight of the body on one side. They practise this, then in pairs they practise fighting without touching It takes some time to persuade some of the boys that this excludes even sly jabs.

If here is a point during any drama lesson when one can say '*Now* they are involved, what came before the lesson is forgotten,' this was that moment, that day. The important thing then was to keep that concentration and that involvement going strong.

In pairs again I get them to move through the hall as before, one being victim and one his pursuer. James Bond music again. They use all the hall, clambering through tunnels of chairs, over the cliff face of the scaffolding. When the record ends each individual lays out on the floor exhausted.

What I should have done next was use a quiet piece of music which they could move freely to in order to relax, as some of the impetus seemed to be lost in stopping dead suddenly.

The last sequence brings together the exercises that have gone before. They change over, chaser and chased, and I tell them that at a certain moment during the music, which they choose themselves, they are to confront one another and use the fighting techniques practised before.

'That was great, Miss, best thing we've done so far.'

I feel exhausted. On the bus again. They are alive. Is this a group of dull, 'B' stream, sec-mod adolescents? They had certainly responded intelligently today. So what was it in this lesson that brought these kids to life?

They are out of the classroom. This is quite simply a change. Routine will never encourage intelligence. They were 'doing'. It was a lively experience, their understanding grew in the moment of feeling. Each individual would make out of the situation what he wished, react in his own way, yet there was an atmosphere of group experience, group understanding. The imaginative power was there before the session, in every member of the class. The emotions were there, the understanding was there. What happened in that session brought out this potential. In drama lessons we are creating the opportunity to think and feel and think again, just as we should be in every other lesson.

The immediacy of drama is its great advantage and it is just this immediacy which is impossible to convey in writing about any session.

So that Wednesday afternoons are over. So many ideas not tried. I regret I did not do the kids justice – I was not adventurous enough. I learnt as much from them, perhaps much more, than they ever learnt from me. I never ceased to be pleased but surprised when they did what I had anticipated or grasped the point, before I had got there myself.

Perhaps because the whole experience was new to her, Valerie has managed better than many experienced or expert practitioners to convey the excitement, the sharing and the renewal that may come through drama. In her dissertation she also explained how it became impossible to isolate what went on at the theatre workshop, how it spilled over into the rest of English, feeding and revitalizing other work. This is often most clearly seen in the impact of mime or improvisation upon pupils' writing: set them to write on 'Disaster at the Mine' and they will perform moderately – according to the way they were led into the writing; spend a period improvising the whole scene in a mining village, involving all the class in particular roles, however, and the impact upon subsequent writing may be remarkable. In the first place, they will probably write twice as much as usual. If the drama has been really successful moreover, one may expect an improvment in quality* as well as quantity: closer visualization and more depth of feeling lead inevitably to a deeper involvement in expressing, in finding words to capture the experience.

I should like to conclude this brief survey by quoting an example of a project carried out by the Devon County Advisory Staff. This involves a team of specialists and the support of the local

*The most striking feature of this being the child's use of words which you didn't think he knew.

resources centre which produced materials for follow-up work in schools. In both manpower and materials, therefore, it is the kind of scheme which no single school would be in a position to replicate. Nevertheless it is deeply suggestive in various ways. Firstly, the principles, though not the scale of the original, are transferable to other situations. Secondly, it may help to break down the assumption that drama relates almost exclusively to English within the secondary curriculum. Thirdly, it suggests the possibilities inherent in an extended dramatic stimulus for initiating group and individual interdisciplinary work very similar to much that is now being attempted in curriculum development schemes. Having seen it in action I can testify to the fact that it *works* both as an experience in itself, and as a starting point for projects of various kinds. The account below is from an explanatory booklet issued to headmasters and staff of schools receiving 'SCAR', the county drama staff's curriculum project.

The Project – Aims

1. To demonstrate how, through educational drama methods and theatre, young people in the fourth and fifth years of their secondary education can be involved deeply in social, economic and political history and to enable teachers to utilise that involvement in subsequent work.

2. To demonstrate how through personal and immediate experience in local environment and history young people can be drawn from the particular concept into the general concepts outlined in (1).

3. To show that first-hand experience and the emotional and intellectual involvement of the whole person is essential in the learning process, and that academic study by itself is a pointless exercise for many unless need and interest are aroused initially by first-hand experience.

4. To illustrate ancillary curriculum possibilities of the theme in terms of arousing interest in minerology and geology, science, biology and ecology in relation to conservation, English, geography, mathematics, religious knowledge, art and music.

5. To link schools and young people with the Dartington Amenities Research Trust and its Field Study Centre at Morwellham in the Tamar Valley, and to encourage residential study visits and the use of the Youth Hostel for that purpose.

The Theme (Warning – Please do not tell youngsters of these plans beforehand)

The day's activities are based on the life of the Devon Great Consolidated Copper Mine in the Tamar Valley between 1844 and 1900. Personalities and events are largely factual, departing only from strict accuracy when the need has arisen to condense diffused and lengthy events or to crystallize attitudes in certain personalities. We believe the spirit and atmosphere of the period to be more important at this stage than a strict attention to detail.

For the first thirty-five minutes the youngsters – up to seventy in number, a maximum teacher–pupil ratio of nine to one – are asked to watch three short scenes* dealing with the decision to begin mining on the Duke of Bedford's land and the effects of that decision in terms of the movement of the farm labourer from an agrarian to an industrial culture.

The youngsters are then split into eight groups for discussion and briefing. Gradually, over the following hour, they are asked to build cottages for themselves and to assume roles as members of farming families in the 1840s – Cobbett's 'hungry forties'. Once the groups have started work in earnest and with a real sense of involvement they are informed that unless they agree to become miners they will be evicted immediately. Three cottages are in any case to be demolished, because the land will be needed for mining. The alternative will be to go to the Workhouse in Tavistock. Stress is laid throughout the day on the youngsters own decision-making within the choices open historically to their characters.

When the above has been resolved an announcement is made that Captain James Phillips, a Mines Manager (one of the team in character) will give a talk illustrated with lantern-slides on mining in the Village Hall. The youngsters then move, still in role as farmers, to a room in the school previously prepared for the talk. A considerable amount of factual information is conveyed with the help of visuals, including an explanation of the system of pitch-bidding at Auctions held by Company representatives.

There is then a break for lunch after which the boys are grouped into three 'pitch-gangs' and the girls into two groups of 'balmaidens'. They are then told that there is a need for a mine and they are invited to build one using rostra, drapes, lighting if available, polystyrene sheets and chairs and tables. This activity is a deliberate use of constructional and creative play at adolescent level; essentially the learning process is much the same as that in operation when a group of infants build a wendy-house for domestic play, although one would not dream of telling them so.

*These are enacted, in costume, by members of the County Drama Staff.

Once the mine has been constructed there is an official opening by Josiah Hitchens, who was the prime mover in forming the DGCM. A pitch auction is then held, with the Mines Manager stating the offered Company price for a pitch; and the pitch gangs, bidding against each other, endeavour to secure a certain number of shillings from the Company in every pound's worth of ore brought up. The pitch gangs are then issued with numbered discs and mining tools and the bal-maidens are instructed in their task of sorting and breaking ore.

There follows an intense period of work as the mine is brought to life by the youngsters and the team, all working 'in role' or in character.

After the mining sequence there is a brief period allowed for them to re-form in family groups to discuss the experience followed by an explanation of a time-jump of roughly twenty years in the life of the mine.

A meeting at Tavistock Town Hall then occurs, with youngsters complaining at a public meeting to the Duke of Bedford and Company representatives about their housing conditions. This is based on an actual petition organized by the Portreeve of Tavistock in the 1860s as a result of the 'revolting and overcrowded living conditions in and around Tavistock'.

At the end of this meeting the miners and their families are informed of the Company's decision to cut the pitch-prices by two-shillings in every pound. They are given time to decide on what action they are to take before a further auction is held.

This last session is open-ended and has always in the past brought a sharp awareness of the need for and consequences of industrial action and the withdrawal of labour. The youngsters are bound by the labour and economic conditions of the time, but the contemporary parallels are obvious and the need for subsequent discussion, research and teaching equally so.

Note

Often violence is near the surface – how can young people experience eviction from their homes and the exploitation of their labour without this happening? The team have structured the day so that if overt violence breaks out there are immediate and effective ways of controlling it – unlike similar situations the youngsters will be facing in adult life.

We make no apologies for this, neither should any be necessary; if young people are *really* going to understand social issues of this kind then they must experience them and their emotions must be engaged as well as their minds. Perhaps through this, understanding and awareness will come – which is what education is about.

The scar is evident today on man's spirit as well as on his environment – the conservation of the land and seas begins with the nurture and conservation of inner values and awarenesses, which is at the root of this project.

Follow-up

Humanities: Much will be self-evident. The mine was producing arsenic in enormous quantities in the last few decades of the nineteenth century, and a great fund of information can be gleaned from the books listed in the bibliography at the end of these notes. Social, political and economic history of period arising from area study.

Timber for baulking imported from North American coast and the Baltic. Exports of copper all over the world. Connection between outbreak of boll-weevil in American cotton plantations and the export of arsenic as insecticide from Morwellham. Study of Tamar and topography of valley. Intensive market-gardening at present and important forestry centre for experimental planting and growth of various timbers.

Minerology/Geology: The Plymouth Caving Society has a great deal of information on this and the profusion of many different minerals in the peninsula from Dartmoor westwards is a fascinating study.

Science/Maths: The entire mine was powered largely by water, with a complex system of pumps, leats (canals) and water-wheels. Total cost of power was £5 per week in 1870. The Cornish Beam-Engine is of course famous in engineering and the Man-Engine used in many mines for carrying men to and from the surface is unique, and would repay research; models could be made. The industrial uses of arsenic and the processing systems used. The system of vertical shafts and addits (horizontal tunnelling) and the methods used, stray into mathematics and trigonometry. The assaying of the ore (Tavistock was the stannary centre for a large area). Systems of blasting and explosives. Methods of baulking, stresses on timber and movement of strata. Maths: systems of payment, pitch-bidding, share-holdings and limited companies, profits made by Duke and shareholders, comparison of wages and prices in 1840, 1870 and 1970.

Biology: The natural history and flora and fauna of the Tamar Valley – a field study trip would be invaluable and the Dartington

Amenities Research Trust will provide information and assistance (address listed at end).

Religious Knowledge: Strong Wesleyan tradition in West Country. Involvement of ministers in social welfare, many Wesleyan hymns used as work-songs by women surface-workers in mine. Attitudes to social conditions affected by religious beliefs. Degree of church-going; importance of church as a relief to the grinding poverty and conditions. Morality and effect of mining on family life. Beer-halls and nightly violence in Gunnislake.

English: Cobbett's *Rural England* – prose-style and generally committed writing. Creative writing in prose and free or formal verse arising out of experience of the drama and the day generally. 'Emotion recollected in tranquillity.' A diary kept by a miner, or his wife, son or daughter.

Frank Booker's excellent work *The Industrial Archaeology of the Tamar Valley* – an author who is as fascinating in his way and on his subject as Gerald Durrell is in his work.

Descriptive work – 'A Shift down the Mine', 'The Day the Bailiff's came'.

Ghosts, pixies, legends and mythology and folklore of Dartmoor and the mines. Orwell's essay – 'Down the Mine'. Oral English and speech work – group discussions, a speech written by a miner for speaking at the Town Hall meeting about housing.

Art: A whole range arising out of the sensory experience of the day itself. The specialist will be better equipped to assess the potential than ourselves. Some tentative suggestions include: Collage and abstract work in two or three dimensions on poverty, hunger down the mine, a miner's home, loss of life and injury, death from typhoid and cholera, etc. Possibly figure work on miners working, women surface-workers, etc.

Music: Group music-making reflecting moods and atmosphere arising from the day's experiences.

Hymns used as work-songs and work-songs (with mimed working?) generally.

The noise and rhythm of the bal-maidens' hammers breaking ore and the miners shovelling, picking and hammering home drills, punctuated by blasting, could provide the basis for melodic percussive music-making in groups or as a class.

The moving quality of a great hymn used on a ceremonial occasion.

Drama: Extension of role-playing in family groupings; recreation of cottage environments, pitch-gang work in mines; exploration of arsenic-producing period in mine; documentary work including songs, original written work and improvised sequences; quotes from source material etc. Movement work in connection with work-song rhythms.

Exploration and research on Tavistock market day, carnival and fair, nature of Gunnislake in 1880s. Mine disaster in Levant Mine.

Improvisation in groups and as a class.

It will be evident immediately that if this project is to succeed in curriculum terms a number of specialist teachers involved in teaching the fourth years should attend the full day and observe.

The presence of the history, geography, English, drama and art specialist teachers is essential and that of the science, maths, music and RE teachers desirable for at least part of the day. (Reproduced by permission of John Butt, Devon County Drama Organizer, and with thanks to all his staff.)

References

Ashton-Warner, S. (1966), *Spinster*, Penguin.

Barnes, D., Britton, J., Rosen, H., and the LATE (1971), *Language, the Learner and the School*, Penguin, rev. edn.

Bereiter, C., and Engelmann, S. (1966), *Teaching Disadvantaged Children in the Pre-School*, Prentice-Hall.

Berger, J. (1968), *A Fortunate Man*, Allen Lane The Penguin Press; Penguin, 1970.

Bernstein, B. (1961), 'Social structure, language and learning', *Educational Research*, vol. 3.

Bernstein, B. (1970), 'A critique of the concept of compensatory education', in D. Rubinstein and C. Stoneman (eds.), *Education for Democracy*, Penguin.

Bernstein, B. (1969), 'A socio-linguistic approach to socialization', in Gumperz and Hymes, *Directions in Sociolinguistics*, Holt, Rinehart & Winston.

Blishen, E. (1966), *Roaring Boys*, Panther.

Bolt, S. (1966), *The Right Response*, Hutchinson.

Brandis, W., and Henderson, D. (1970), *Social Class, Language and Communication*, Routledge & Kegan Paul.

Britton, J. (1967), *Talking and Writing*, Methuen.

Britton, J. (1970), *Language and Learning*, Allen Lane The Penguin Press; Penguin, 1972.

Brown, R. (1958), *Words and Things,* Free Press.

Bruner, J. S. (1966), *Studies in Cognitive Growth*, Wiley.

Cazden, C. B. (1967), 'On individual differences in language competence and performance', *Journal of Special Education*, vol. 1, no. 2, pp. 135–50.

Channon, G. (1968), 'Language teaching in a Harlem school', *Urban Rev.*, February.

Chomsky, N. (1964), 'Formal discussion of *The Development of Grammar in Child Language* by W. Miller and S. Ervin', Society for Research in Child Development monographs, no. 29, pp. 34–9.

Clegg, A., and Megson, B. (1968), *Children in Distress*, Penguin.

Clements, S. (1967), 'Film making and the English lesson', *English in Education*, vol. 1, no. 1.

Creber, J. W. P. (1968), *Sense and Sensitivity*, University of London Press.

Department of Education and Science (1968), *Drama*, Education survey 2, HMSO

Deutsch, M., Maliver, Brown and Cherry (1964), 'Communication of information in the elementary school classroom', Institute for Developmental Studies, New York Medical College. Summarized in M. Deutsch, *The Disadvantaged Child*, Basic Books, 1967, ch. 10.

Dixon, J. (1969), *Growth through English*, Oxford University Press.

Douglas, J. W. B. (1964), *The Home and the School*, MacGibbon & Kee; Panther, 1972.

Ervin-Tripp, S. (1966), 'Language development', in M. L Hoffman and L. W. Hoffman (eds.), *Review of Child Development Research*, Russell Sage Foundation.

Fader, D., and McNeil, E. B. (1969), *Hooked on Books*, Pergamon.

Fuchs, E. (1966), *Pickets at the Gate*, Free Press.

Haggitt, T. (1967), *Working with Language*, Blackwell.

Halliday, M. A. K. (1968), 'Language and experience', *Educational Review*, vol. 20, no. 2.

Halliday, M. A. K. (1968), 'Language and experience', *Educational Review*, vol. 22. no. 1, pp. 34–6.

Hannam, C., Smyth, P., and Stephenson, N. (1971), *Young Teachers and Reluctant Learners*, Penguin.

Harrington, M. (1963), *The Other America*, Penguin.

Herndon, J. (1968), *The Way it Spozed to Be*, Pitman.

Hess, R. D., and Shipman, V. C. (1965), 'Early experience and the socialization of the cognitive modes in children', *Child Development*, vol. 36, no. 4, pp. 881–3. Reprinted in R. J. Havinghurst and B. L. Neugarten (eds.), *Society and Education*, Allyn & Bacon, 1967.

Hymes, D. (1967), 'Models of the interaction of language and social setting', *Journal of Social Issues*, no. 22.

Hymes, D. (1968), 'On communicative competence', in S. Diamond (ed.), *Anthropological Approaches to Education*.

Jones, R. M. (1968), *Fantasy and Feeling in Education*, University of London Press; Penguin, 1972.

Klein, J. (1965), *Samples from English Cultures*, Routledge & Kegan Paul.

Kohl, H. (1968), *36 Children*, Gollancz; Penguin, 1971.

Kohl, H. (1969), *The Open Classroom*, Methuen.

Langer, S. (1958), 'The cultural importance of the arts', in M. F. Andrews (ed.), *Aesthetic Form and Education*, Syracuse University Press.

Lawton, D. (1968), *Social Class, Language and Education*, Routledge & Kegan Paul.

Lesser, P. 1969), English for the slow learner', *Use of English*, vol. 21, no. 1.

Luria, A. R. and Yudovich, F. Ia. (1959), *Speech and the Development of Mental Processes in the Child*, Staples Press; Penguin, 1971.

McCarthy, D. (1954), 'Language developments in children', in L. Carmichael (ed.), *Manual of Child Psychology*, Wiley.

Mackenzie, R. F. (1970), *State School*, Penguin.

Morris, B. (1969), Response to G. H. Bantock's 'Conflicts of values in teacher education', in *Towards a Policy for the Education of Teachers*, Butterworth.

Oakeshott, M. (1959), *The Voice of Poetry in the Conversation of Mankind*, Bowes & Bowes.

Postman, N., and Weingartner, C. (1969), *Teaching as a Subversive Activity*, Delacorte Press; Penguin, 1971.

Robertson, G. (1969), ATM Supplement, November.

Rogers, C. (1967), *On Becoming a Person*, Constable.

Rosenthal, R., and Jacobson, L. (1968), *Pygmalion in the Classroom: Teacher Expectation and the Pupil's Intellectual Ability*, Holt, Rinehart & Winston.

Sampson, O. (1966), 'Reading and adjustment: a review of the literature', *Educational Research*, vol. 8, no. 3.

School of Barbiana (1970), *Letter to a Teacher*, Penguin.

Schools Council (1967), *Society and the Young School Leaver*, Working paper no. 11, HMSO.

Searle, C. (1971), *Stepney Words*, Reality Press.

Spinley, B. M. (1953), *The Deprived and the Privileged*, Routledge & Kegan Paul.

Stenhouse, L. (1968), 'The Humanities curriculum project', *Journal of Curriculum Studies*, vol. 1, no. 1.

Stenhouse, L. (1969), Article in *New Society*, 24 July.

Wells, H. G. (1910), *History of Mr Polly*, Longman.

Whitehead, F. (1966), *The Disappearing Dais*, Chatto & Windus.

Wilkinson, A. (1971), *The Foundations of Language*, Oxford University Press.

Young, M. and McGeeney, P. (1968), *Learning Begins at Home*, Routledge & Kegan Paul.

Select Bibliography

D. Barnes, J. Britton, H. Rosen and the LATE, *Language, the Learner and the School*, Penguin, 1971, rev. edn.

*J. Britton, *Language and Learning*, Allen Lane The Penguin Press, 1970; Penguin, 1972.

*J. S. Bruner, *Studies in Cognitive Growth*, Wiley, 1966.

*John P. de Cecco, *The Psychology of Language, Thought and Instruction: A Collection of Readings*, Holt, Rinehart & Winston, 1963.

*S. Ervin-Tripp, 'Language development', in M. L. Hoffman and L. W. Hoffman (eds.), *Review of Child Development Research*, vol. 2, Russel Sage Foundation, N.Y.

F. Flower, *Language and Education*, Longman, 1966.

C. Hannam, P. Smythe and N. Stephenson, *Young Teachers and Reluctant Learners*, Penguin, 1971.

P. Herriot, *An Introduction to the Psychology of Language*, Methuen, 1970.

A. Jones and J. Mulford (eds.), *Children using Language*, Oxford University Press, 1972.

R. Jones, *Fantasy and Feeling in Education*, University of London Press, 1968; Penguin, 1972.

Suzanne Langer, *Philosophy in a New Key*, Harvard University Press, 1957.

*D. Lawton, *Social Class, Language and Education*, Routledge & Kegan Paul, 1968.

A. R. Luria and F. Ia. Yudovich, *Speech and the Development of Mental Processes in the Child*, Staples Press, 1969; Penguin, 1971.

*D. McCarthy, 'Language development in children', in L. Carmichael (ed.), *Manual of Child Psychology*, Wiley, 1954.

Carl R. Rogers, *On Becoming a Person*, Constable, 1967.

B. M. Spinley, *The Deprived and the Privileged*, Routledge & Kegan Paul, 1953.

L. S. Vygotsky, *Thought and Language*, MIT Press and Wiley, 1962.

*A. Wilkinson, *The Foundations of Language*, Oxford University Press, 1971.

Books marked * contain particularly useful bibliographies.